Awards 35:

Hunger & Thirst

Nimrod International Journal

Awards 35:
Hunger & Thirst

Nimrod International Journal is indexed in
Humanities International Complete

ISBN: 978-0-9860178-2-7   ISSN: 0029-053X
Volume 57, Number 1
Fall/Winter 2013

THE UNIVERSITY OF TULSA — TULSA, OKLAHOMA

This Awards issue is dedicated to Joan Flint,
poet, patron of the arts, and constant friend of Nimrod.
Joan served as poetry editor for many years.
Her discernment and love of literature and everything
that blooms are an example for us all.

Poetry Workshop

Do stay in class and listen to me read.
Will my metaphor speak and grow for you?
You are kind and smile. You look around to
See what others think. You shuffle your feet.
Now you read yours . . . and I wonder what you need . . .
Some praise perhaps. Are you the one who
Stayed up late and wrote in blood? Thoughts this new
Are raw and rough, they need more time.
                                  Indeed,
This world is rough. It will pick apart
Our verses without our even asking it.
We do ourselves no favor to be still.
Quality declines in quiet. Take heart—
Hold the poems firm; dissect them bit
By bit. Friends should do what strangers always will.

—Joan Flint
Nimrod Journal,
Vol, 19, No. 1

ADVISORY BOARD

Acknowledgements

This issue of *Nimrod* is funded by donations, subscriptions, and sales. *Nimrod* and The University of Tulsa acknowledge with gratitude the many individuals and organizations that support *Nimrod*'s publication, annual prize, and outreach programs: *Nimrod*'s Advisory and Editorial Boards; and *Nimrod*'s Angels, Benefactors, Donors, and Patrons.

Angel ($1,000+)
: Ellen and Steve Adelson, Margery Bird, Joan Flint, George Krumme, Susan and Robert Mase, The Ruth K. Nelson Trust, Ann Daniel Stone, The Jill and Robert Thomas Charitable Fund, Mary Lee Townsend and Burt Holmes, Randi and Fred Wightman, The John Steele Zink Foundation

Benefactor ($500+)
: Ivy and Joseph Dempsey, Stephani Franklin, Bruce Kline, Harry Potter, Lisa Ransom and David Flesher, Fran Ringold, The Kathleen Patton Westby Foundation, Jane Wiseman

Donor ($100+)
: Teresa and Alex Adwan, Harvey Blumenthal, Colleen Boucher, Diane Burton, Katherine and John Coyle, TD Design, Marion and William Elson, Nancy and Raymond Feldman, Ken Fergeson, Sherri and Stuart Goodall, E. Ann Graves, Cynthia Gustavson, Ellen Hartman, Nancy and William Hermann, Linda Jennings, Carol Johnson, Elizabeth and Sam Joyner, The Kerr Foundation, Therese Young Kim, Marjorie and David Kroll, Lydia Kronfeld, Robert LaFortune, Roberta Marder, James McGill, Carol McGraw, Connie Murray, Catherine Gammie Nielsen, Lynne and John Novack, Donna O'Rourke and Tom Twomey, Nancy and Thomas Payne, Pamela Pearce, Judy and Roger Randle, Andrea Schlanger, Joan and Harry Seay, Diane and James Seebass, Fran and Bruce Tibbetts, Renata and Sven Treitel, Peter Walter, Melissa and Mark Weiss, Ruth and Kenneth Weston, Joy Whitman, Penny Williams, Josephine Winter, Mary Young and Joseph Gierek

Patron ($50+)
: Helen and M. E. Arnold, Margaret and Charles Audrain, Mary Cantrell and Jason Brimer, Kimberly Doenges, Kay and F. Daniel Duffy, Linda and William Epperson, Joann and Robert Franzen, Britton Gildersleeve, William Kellough, Leslie and Chris Matthies, Geraldine McLoud, Taylor and Joshua Parish, Linda and Bruce Stoesser, Krista and John Waldron, Ann Watson, Patricia Wheeler

TABLE OF CONTENTS

Editor's Note: "Hunger & Thirst:"
Not Goodbye But Hungering for a Bit More and Less

Lasting matters, and so does a new record. It was 1966 when Professor Winston Weathers offered me the opportunity to clean out a filing cabinet, taller than I, filled with unread submissions for *Nimrod*, filled with discoveries yet to be made, for opportunities for me to develop discernment and best of all, make new friends—and some enemies, of course. For no matter how discreet, a rejection is a rejection! I first met Winston in the 1950s when he lived in the apartment above mine with his partner, Joseph Nichols. Winston was trying to make a living as a poet and fiction writer; I was trying to be a dutiful wife and mother to a ten-day-old baby and tinkering once in a while with my own writing. By 1966 Winston had obtained a Ph.D. and was a professor at TU, eager to pass on the editorship of *Nimrod*. I had gained three more children, three of them now in school, and I was eager to take on new challenges. Happily already teaching just two courses, I couldn't resist the lure of the unknown, a literary magazine with a circulation of 225, but with great promise. Despite never having been larger than 32 pages, folded and stapled, even by 1966 *Nimrod* had already published not only local authors like 17-year-old Ted Berrigan (later associated with the famed New York School of writers) but also Lewis Ginsberg, William Stafford, and other national figures. Small, even very small literary journals have always been the backbone of American literature. Everyone knew everyone in those days and by phone, direct mail, and in person—they came to *Nimrod*.

The friends I made through association with *Nimrod* seem a name-dropper's delight: not only William Stafford, but Denise Levertov, W. S. Merwin, and many others slept at my house (in the guest room) and became life-long friends. Those were the days when we couldn't afford to spend money on hotels for our guests, so others in Tulsa also have fond memories of sleep-overs.

This year, we selected for Volume 56, Number 2, *Lasting Matters: Writers 57 and Over*, the most successful issue in recent history, some of the friends and associates we had made over the years, including U.S. Poet Laureate Ted Kooser and Pulitzer Prize-winner Stephen Dunn, but also new writers in their 70's and over who have grown up knowing about *Nimrod* and eagerly responded to our call to the seasoned and lively.

And for this year's Awards 35, Volume 57, with the help of a bit of serendipity and a good deal of astute selection, we upheld the senior trend with a second prize winner in poetry who is 74, and fulfilled *Nimrod*'s mission of discovery with the selection of a young writer of 24 as First-Prize winner. In fiction too, we have the experienced and the new, not just among the winners but among the Honorable Mentions and finalists.

In every issue, we publish material submitted "over-the-transom," a term from the past referring to unsolicited submissions which arrive as if thrown over or through an open transom. These submissions have gone through the rigorous process of selection, but were not submitted for the *Nimrod* Awards, a choice that each author makes for him or herself. Selection for publication is of course an award in itself, but we wanted to find a method of calling attention to what we feel to be the most outstanding of these. In this issue, Bipin Aurora's story "The Lovers of Bengal," in which the narrator hungers for traditional family connections, and Bonnie Wailee Kwong's poetry in which the passion to connect is not only personal but weds science and math within its cartography, hold particular fascination for me. In the future, I would like to see *Nimrod* have a way of recognizing outstanding general submissions, not in the form of a regularly awarded prize, as with the Pablo Neruda and Katherine Anne Porter competitions, but in a less formal and more spontaneous way, to reflect the serendipitous surprises such submissions present.

But that is for Eilis O'Neal to tell you about, for she will be an able and lasting leader, with her generous spirit and scrupulously honed abilities. After all, she has been with us since she was 18; she is now 32, just one year older than I was when Winston lured me into this adventure in publishing. My simple task is only to say thank you for putting up with me these 47 years. I welcome my future job as Senior Advisory Editor, which, like being a grandmother, means that I get to do what I want to do.

Editor's Note: Awards 35: Hunger & Thirst

Every spring, life at *Nimrod* revolves around the reading and selection of the contest manuscripts sent in for the *Nimrod* Literary Awards. Forty-one editors and two student interns spend months opening, sorting, and reading thousands of fiction and poetry manuscripts. We consider and evaluate, and sometimes argue over, each one, until we have a carefully selected group of finalists to send to our final judges, this year the renowned Cristina García and Aimee Nezhukumatathil. It's hard work, but that means the payoff when we find a finalist is even sweeter. In fact, there's sometimes happy shouting involved when a great manuscript is uncovered, evidence, you might say, that we hunger for that thrill of discovery.

Which leads me to the second task given to our editors as they read: the selection of an issue theme. Unlike the spring issue, the fall Awards issue has no theme when it is announced. And yet, through happy serendipity, we always seem to find a common thread winding its way through the work of our winners, honorable mentions, finalists, and semi-finalists. This year, that theme is *Hunger and Thirst*.

What is hunger? What is thirst? In the literary world, it's often more than a rumbling in the belly or a dryness in the throat. Hunger and thirst represent the things we most desperately want, the desires and longings of our innermost selves. Sometimes they're what we most need, sustenance for the mind, body, and soul; yet, sometimes what we want most isn't what's good for us. In this issue, you'll find poems and stories that reveal many sorts of hungers and many sorts of thirsts, whether expressed humorously or seriously, baldly or covertly, in our own time or in times past.

Our four Award winners delve into hunger and thirst, each in a different way. Perhaps the most overt depiction of hunger comes in Jacob M. Appel's Second-Prize-winning story, "Paracosmos." Here, a young girl loses a best friend, and in her deep desire for another she creates one, a girl who may or may not be, as her mother discovers, imaginary. Kristina Gorcheva-Newberry's First-Prize-winning story, "Boys on the Moskva River," features a narrator consumed by the alternating need to live up to and escape his older brother's dangerous legacy. A blacksmith in First-Prize poetry winner Sarah Crossland's "Rakkaus" longs for a wife, going so far as to create a "tin and copper bride" in his loneliness. And Lynn Shoemaker tries to fight against the hunger for answers in the face of natural disaster in his Second-Prize-winning poem "Survivor Ocean, Suicide Sea" with the mantra of "I shall not want. I shall not want."

The theme continues in all its permutations with our honorable mentions, finalists, and semi-finalists, as well as with the writers selected through our general submission process throughout the year. A longing for the dead forms the backbone of many poems, as Matthew Thorburn speaks to his "almost" daughter in "The Light that Lasts All Summer," wishing that he could show her "what life is like in all its dizzying minutiae, the simple everydayness" of New York City, and Jude Nutter uses poetry to show us "where the dead go" in "Still Life with Full Moon and Ibis."

The desire for love is found throughout these pages, both when it is fulfilled, as in Katherine Bode-Lang's "In Drought, in Rain" and when it is just a memory, as in Geffrey Davis's "What Returns."

Sometimes it is nature itself that is ravenous, as in Julie Taylor's "Hungry Lake," where "locals say the lake is hungry."

An Afghani girl thirsts to belong both to her cultural heritage and to her new American home in Alison Moore's "Safe House," while the hunger for safety itself permeates Sandra Hunter's "Angel in Glasgow" as a young Sudanese refugee tries to survive on the streets.

Rosalind Pace explores the sometimes ephemeral quality of our hopes and yearnings in "Wanting to Read Sanskrit," wondering if we could invent a language "to speak of what we long for." And Janet McNally reinvents one of the best known stories about hunger in her poem "Gretel, After."

And this is just the beginning. Indeed, while you might say that all writing is, to some degree, about hunger and thirst, the varied approaches to the theme in this issue show a remarkable breadth of creativity, thoughtfulness, playfulness, and skill. Make up a mug of hot cocoa and put a few cookies on a plate—no reading on an empty stomach here!—and come feasting with us.

❊ ❊ ❊

If I may end with a short personal note: As Fran mentioned, I first became involved with *Nimrod* as a work-study student during my freshman year at TU. I recently realized that this means that I've spent more than a third of my life as a part of this journal. When I was just eighteen years old, it offered me, a nervous undergrad, a way to break into the literary world I desperately wanted to be a part of, and it has continued to offer me—as it offers so many—a refuge filled with the creativity and community of readers and writers.

Fran is a tough—if not impossible—act to follow as Editor of *Nimrod*. But I'm looking forward to continuing and expanding my service to a journal that has given me so much. Thank you for joining me.

Hunger & Thirst . . .

Eleanor Leonne Bennett, photograph

Safranschou

Hundreds of years ago, a man in Germany
was burned on a pyre of his own fake saffron
according to the forgery laws of the land.

They caught me mixing
silk threads with beet and empty-
flavored stamens
and this is my punishment:

The fire blooms me.

Flames secret
as a crocus unleashing
its first color
in challenge to the bruise-
pushed dawn.

I know there must be counterfeits
for beauty—

Not sunrose.
Not valentine, not dame
of the heart. If I say red
you will think of existing

flowers but I am trying to name
the color developing
into my hands. From my wrists
roped to the prison pole,
where skin sheeting
holds on as if tethered
with only a song.

You cannot know how colors
chime until you listen —

The red inside
a mother's skirt,
bloodberry. A throated
loon feather if birds could be made
of mostly smoke.

In time I will be
made of mostly smoke.

If this is dying —
all my calm
bones slowly being let out,
eroded to, their hollows
confessed — then let me have it,
let me call it beautiful.

Lots

In Irish legend, Macha's husband boasts to the king
of her godliness — how she can canter, outlast the wind's
last breaths, even when she's with child.

The king's heralds arrive in léines and cloaks
to announce a necessary contest: I will race

the horses. So my stomach spins as if its own
stormy planet — motherhood and sport, to them,

are reversible as night and nightmare. They drag me
to the starting block with all the Clydesdales

and the thoroughbreds that they can gather —
twenty-seven tame or wild horses, and me, Macha,

a competitive animal. The truth is even the gods
are afraid of challenges, and when the start-flag takes

the shape of a shrub in the dirt, out of love
for winning, there go my lungs, pink nets cast —

they bring my rivals closer to me. I can overtake
their haunches, every stallion. The sun puts eyes

of light in their pelts and dust, thick as brume, hides
for my teeth. Without thinking of my body

for what it carries — through the pains of pretending
to be human — I win. Here at the finish,

beneath their cauls, my new children wail.
There was a little town of bones in my feet

and it is pillaged now. My son runs to the sea.
My daughter, standing, folds and dresses me.

Rakkaus

*Spoken by the Smith Ilmarinen,
from the Finnish epic,* The Kalevala

In the thirteenth hour, I climb out from the fire
room, soot-blushed, stripping off each

retardant mitt, my apron hung in a heavy shadow
over the back of a chair. This is my gallery

of smitten things: armor, jugs and mazers,
batch knives stamped with the sun's open mouth.

I once cast the sky and its stray colors but where
is my luck for a wife? The dead won't listen

to our wishing anymore. If they did, I would ask
for a woman to grow orchids with — unmetal

and cautionless. A garden as real as a breath.
The old words tell us that if we can't find

love under the rocks and in the maze-
topped moss, we must fashion it ourselves

from all the loose tools and parts we live with.
So I gather a kerchief of coins from the sea

and bring them to heat on the plane of my forge.
The andiron sturdy as a ribcage, smoking.

The hammer in my hand: let it make loveliness.
Alloy cheeks, lids rose-dulled, curls vagrant

as a chandelier. My tin and copper bride,
I have hoped for one whose shape you echo.

Each roak and seam tells a scar as long
as a silver river, and had you working arms

or feet, I know you would step closer—
still without a mouth to kiss me. You can't

design desire but, starting with emptiness,
perhaps it can be learned. On the floor

of swarf and coils, the unattended clock-
shards of your heart quit their sounds.

The places where your eyes could be
quiet as the infinite bending of a cup.

Steve Lautermilch, photograph

Clavilux

*In the 1920s, Thomas Wilfred invented an eighth
art form, "Lumia," or the sculpture of light itself.*

In the story of the theft
of fire, Prometheus — bone-disguiser,
wanton maker of masks —
announces to the humans the first
fennel-stalk torch
of light. Flame tight
and final as a handshake,
tumbling the scent of burnt anise —
everything original must first,
in some way, be taken
from the gods. And not only
in the myths. Here, too, we steal
the eighty-six colors common
to this world from the light
organ — blush threads,
dark perse, loosely woven ibis
feather. As the night
lengthens, into our purses
and pockets, the canteens of cupped
hands: a flicker of pale
honey, topaz, wheat,
and out of cloud — water balled
into a greener shield —
every tint of dew that could magnify
a blade of mountain grass.
For our safekeeping,
until we can retrieve them later.
The eye, such a numinous thief,
saccading with the long
white tremor of the concert violin.

Boys on the Moskva River

When my brother died in the winter of 1998, the snow fell all night and all day and all the following week, so they didn't find him right away, the contour of his body barely delineated but otherwise indistinguishable from the shrouded, ice-etched forms. Out the window of my brother's luxurious apartment, the Moskva River appeared frozen, layered in white as though bandaged with strips of gauze. But if you stared at it long enough, if you let your eyes adjust to the ossifying whiteness all around, you could see the river tremble and shift underneath the snow, wet and sunken and hollow in the middle like a puncture wound.

"We need to find your father," my mother said, filling her cup with more coffee. "He can help carry the casket."

"You need to eat something, Mom," I said, turning away from the window that still held the misty imprint of my hand. "Really. You don't sleep, you don't eat. You'll get sick."

She peered into her coffee, her forehead strained with wrinkles, eyes squinting hard as though she was trying to read her fortune in the impervious blackness of the cup.

Our father left us two months before my birth. He didn't find another woman, and he didn't hate our mother or his two-year-old son, who was always sick and crying and not sleeping. But our father wanted to be free, free like a bird. If he had wings, he'd told my mother, he would fly away. But he had legs, and so he walked and didn't come back, his fate a mystery.

"Somewhere, in the old phonebook, there's his parents' number and address. Perhaps he's there," my mother said.

"What will I say to him? Your older son is dead, and even though you haven't seen him for twenty-six years, asshole, we need you to be a pallbearer? And what about me, Mom? Technically, he's my father too."

She didn't respond, her face buried in her hands. She wasn't old, although right there and then, she could've been a grandmother, dressed in a stretched dark-brown sweater, with her gray hair swept behind her ears, frail, sunless skin, shoulders weighed low from the years of servitude—to her parents, to us, to my brother.

"It isn't about you, Leova," she breathed out the words.

"It's never about me. But always about him. Tell you what, Mom, he didn't care about us. He preferred the city, the streets, to his family. He was just like our father."

Again, she didn't respond, her eyes tracing after a covey of flurries spinning webs behind the window glass. Somewhere, in the yard, there was my brother's shoe, buried under a heap of snow.

❊ ❊ ❊

The year is 1980; I'm eight and my brother Konstantin is ten. It's one of the hottest summers we've had. There's no rain and there's no wind. The sun is a pyre in the sky, a blazing vessel of ceaseless heat. The air is dry and brittle; it tingles on your lips. Every living thing, every bug, every leaf pines for rain. The grass sighs and turns to dust, the flowers shrivel by mid-morning, the trees offer little shade and no reprieve. They don't move or sway their branches or rustle their leaves but stand still as though painted on a piece of paper; the colors waver and melt away.

We're swimming in the Moskva River, my brother and I, and he teaches me how to float on my back. Dragonflies dapple the surface, pinpricks of golden light, and for a moment, Konstantin disappears and I'm left alone, drifting softly, limbs akimbo. I feel his arms wrap around my chest and yank me underwater so quickly the sun shrinks to the size of a fist, and then all is dark and murky, a pillar of silt rising from the bottom. I hold my breath for as long as I can, until Konstantin lets go and I push through the water, climbing higher and higher, guided by the trembling rings of light.

"Fight for your life, little brother," he says as soon as I shoot out. "Because no one else will."

I flounder and suck air and paddle ashore with all my strength.

Our mother is home, doing laundry or frying fish; she doesn't know we've gone to the river or that I've almost drowned. She worries about Konstantin being too thin, squirming like a worm out of her loving arms. I'm too heavy for my age, thick and sturdy, a stump of a boy.

❄   ❄   ❄

On the day of the funeral, the cemetery was a giant cocoon of snow, with monuments poking here and there and tall three-barred crosses. From afar, they resembled crippled frozen birds caught midflight. The gaunt trees stood crystalized-white, the limbs gave an impression of being broken and soldered to the trunks at odd angles. It was impossible to detect where snow ended and clouds began, all fused together, the sky and the earth and the thin whitish air like a muslin cloth suspended on trees and threaded through our fingers. The four of us agreed to be pallbearers—me, our neighbor, and two of Konstantin's friends. The casket felt heavy, heavier than I'd expected, as though the snow, too, had added to the weight of Konstantin's body. My father didn't wish to attend the funeral or speak to my mother, and he didn't call me by my name during our short conversation. Right before hanging up, he said, "Your brother, was he mean to you? You two must've got into a lot of fights."

"Some," I had replied. "Some fights."

The grave wasn't long enough, and we waited, shivering but otherwise not moving, as the gravediggers hacked and chopped away. The sounds of their shovels and pickaxes shook the dumb earth and my mother's shoulders. Every now and then, I would glance at her stooping under the weight of the sheepskin coat Konstantin had bought for her last year. The coat seemed two sizes too big, or she two sizes too small, wilted inside its dyed-black fur so that only the tips of her ungloved fingers were left visible and her face, like a frost-bitten apple, dark and lonely. Once, she'd seemed tall and proud to us, indomitable, with a broad, sturdy back eager to support our weight and carry us into the future. But with years, as we thrived, she withered, as though she had given us not only her energy and her labor, but her skin, her hair, her blood, all of her vital powers. We were like vampires who couldn't control their urges, seduced by the sight and smell of such tender, familiar flesh, and who kept gorging on her life to sustain their own.

My mother had decided not to cremate the body and not to open the casket, even though Konstantin's face wasn't mangled; the first bullet had entered his heart and the second the back of his head, becoming trapped, permanently lodged inside his brain. For years afterward, I would dream about it—him sauntering down the street, whistling a Beatles song, "All the Lonely People" or "Yellow Submarine," shooting spit between his teeth and raising the collar of his leather coat like an American-movie gangster, like someone for whom death meant no more than a change of scenery or a new costume. I imagined the hitman too, screwing a silencer onto his gun, loitering behind a building, aiming the gun first at the distant sprawl of trees, then at my brother's back, then at his head, his broom-bristle hair always cropped so short. Occasionally, in my dreams, it would be me trudging toward Konstantin's apartment complex, awaiting the bullet to enter my skull and tear into the cerebral cortex, and I would feel it tunnel through the lobes—occipital, parietal, frontal, temporal—nestling into my thalamus or even not sinking that deep, segueing into the furrow between the two hemispheres. I would wake up drenched in cold sweat, cradling the back of my head, expecting to find the bullet hole, the raw ugly edges of the wound.

❊ ❊ ❊

The year is 1984, the last winter before *perestroika*. We're twelve and fourteen, and we're shopping for groceries—milk, eggs, beef cutlets rolled in breadcrumbs that crunch between our teeth after our mother has fried them in butter, or rather sunflower oil, but we don't know it then because everything tastes like butter, rich, delicious. The grocery store is invaded by people who scour the half-empty aisles, foraging for food, plucking off the shelves anything they can spot, be it a soup-pack of bones and gamy meat or sprouted purple-eyed potatoes. We've been warned that the country's supply of flour will peter out in less than a month. But as boys, we don't really know how long a month is, how short. Konstantin strays off hoping to procure beef cutlets while I'm ordered to guard two bottles of milk, a bag of millet, a can of herring, and half a loaf of black bread.

It's been a while since Konstantin has left, and my arms begin to tingle from heat. I untie my earflaps and take my rabbit hat off; my hair is wet, sticking to my scalp. Herds of people jostle by, but Konstantin isn't among them, and I begin to panic, a lump of fear swelling in my stomach. I abandon the tote on the floor, just for a minute, I think, and scuttle toward the meat department; my brother isn't there but a few older women are haggling over pig's feet to boil for *xolodets*. It suddenly occurs to me that perhaps Konstantin has already gone home, and I weave through the crowd, pushing between the heavy doors, a cloud of snow in my face.

I'm almost back to our dingy graffiti-scarred apartment building when I hear him whistle behind my back.

"Hey," he says. "Dick-head, where're you going? And where are all the groceries? Where's the bag?"

I halt, my heart nudged tight between my ribs, and I think about my mother reaching into the chicken's cavity that morning and yanking out the slimy pebble-shaped organ, then rinsing it in cold water and frying it in oil.

"Quit being such a baby," Konstantin says. "Stop the fuck crying and wipe that snot. Disgusting." He's tall and wiry, with a mean cleft in his chin he's already begun to shave, not because he has hair, but because he wants it to grow faster.

"You disappeared," I say, sniffling, shielding my face with my sleeve. "You left me for an hour."

"I said I was coming back. And I did, didn't I?" He pulls a *chekushka* of vodka out of the pocket and unscrews the lid, takes a long hard swig; it's the first time I see him doing something forbidden, something adult.

❊ ❊ ❊

In a crowd of friends and family at the cemetery, I noticed a young woman with a little boy, three or four at the most, bundled up in a down coat and with a red scarf noosing his neck and mouth. He fidgeted with the scarf, pushing it down, but the mother pulled it back up, making sure the boy's face stayed swaddled at all times. The young woman kept her eyes on the casket while the red-scarfed boy rolled a snowball between his tiny gloved hands; both the mother and the child stood closer to the trees than to the grave, separate from the rest of the mourners. After the burial, she didn't follow the crowd toward the gates but moved behind the thicket of trees until all I could discern was a small patch of red flashing in the distance like a bullfinch or some other scarlet-breasted bird.

Weeks would pass before I would see them again, weeks filled with silence, more snow, and mounds of tedious paperwork concerning the inheritance. My father had contacted us a few times

insisting on his share, but we ignored his impertinent demands.
Soon we became privy to Konstantin's bank account, as well as his
ritzy apartment, where my mother and I relocated. She wanted to
be as close to her son in death as she couldn't be in life. She moved
about the five richly furnished rooms of his home silently, like a
ghost, fading into the forms and shapes of his life, the pearl-inlaid
tables and curvy velour couches and solid oak bookcases, with
shelves upon shelves of American movies: *The Godfather*, *Goodfel-
las*, *Prizzi's Honor*, *Once Upon a Time in America*, *The Terminator*, *Die
Hard*. My mother sat in her son's soft cherry suede chairs and lay
in his field-wide bed, refusing to strip off his sheets. She fingered
his clothes—jeans and cashmere sweaters and expensive leather
jackets—and lingered by the tall velvet-draped windows, her quiet
presence often unnoticed yet somehow palpable, like a sudden
breath of warm air on the nape of your neck. I bought groceries
and cooked most mornings before work, but she would forget to
eat it, forget there was life after life, hers after Konstantin's. She
became so thin, threadbare, you could see through her, could see
her heart pulsing slower and slower, enmeshed in silence and grief.
I had her all to myself now, and yet she was slipping away, dissi-
pating into the darkness.

As for me, I enjoyed living in my brother's apartment. I put
on his flamboyant, if a bit arrogant, lifestyle like an ill-fitting glove
of oiled, supple leather; it stretched with wear and gave a nice
shape to the hand. I could now continue my education, as opposed
to managing a small food-and-liquor kiosk for the rest of my life,
and enjoy the view of the city and the Moskva River while eating
my meals, gazing dreamily out the snow-brushed window. There
was darkness out there, and there was light, the city quilt patched
with shadows. The outside world was like the river itself—treacherous and invisible, protected by snow that would soon melt,
exposing deep cracks in the ice, through which the water would try
to escape, gain a semblance of freedom.

When the doorbell rang, I was loading the dishwater, and my
mother had dozed off in Konstantin's desk chair, a picture album
hugged against her belly. I recognized the woman and the boy
from the cemetery and felt obliged to ask them in, nodding and
stooping, awkwardly, as though I were the one who had appeared
on their doorstep with a stern, urgent gaze and a clump of snow
underfoot. The young woman had a smooth face, small

inconspicuous features, except maybe for the mouth—too broad, too pulpy, intimidating. She said nothing while she undressed the boy, hanging his red scarf and coat on the hall tree. Squatting, she pulled off his boots one by one before producing a pair of fuzzy slippers from a backpack. She fitted them on his feet, set the boots next to mine by the door, then got up and squeezed the boy in her arms, his sweet scared face nuzzled into her fur coat.

"He's your nephew," she said and pushed the little guy toward me with such a force he bumped against my hip.

"What do you mean he's my nephew? Who are you?"

"Unimportant. But you must take care of him because I can't, not at the moment."

"No way. You fucking kidding me?"

With her sad, dark eyes she studied my sweater—or, rather, Konstantin's—gray with purple stripes. It was a little too snug and long in the sleeves, but I loved how soft it felt against my chapped, wintered skin. "I bought it for him," she finally said.

"That doesn't prove squat."

"No?"

"Konstantin hated children. Compared them to asshole hairs, dirty and annoying."

"I really must go. But I'll be back. I promise."

"When?"

She shrugged. "Soon. Be good to him. He'll eat anything and he's stranger-friendly." She opened the door and walked out, scurried down the steps with dull thuds. I stared at the puddle of water on the floor, and then at the boy. He didn't move, half-leaning against me, his kitten-gray eyes brimming with tears.

"Shit," I said.

"Shit," he echoed.

※ ※ ※

The year is 1988; the day after my high school graduation. The sky is drifting with clouds changing shapes—houses to cars, cars to wheels, wheels to breasts. Mountainous, doughy, with soft areolas and long sugary nipples. All of them are, of course, too high to reach, but I keep tasting them, keep smacking my virgin lips while Konstantin is in the other room, having sex with one of his beautiful girlfriends. He's never at home anymore, comes to sleep occasionally or visits when our mother is out, so he doesn't have to answer her questions: Where are you all day? What do you eat? Where did you get that leather jacket?

There are no sounds coming from the room, but as I press my palms and my face, my cheeks, my nose, my tongue, all of me to the wall, I imagine their bodily vibrations, gentle thrusts growing steadier and harder as my penis engorges with blood, about to spill. My hand reaches inside my shorts when the door swings open and my brother's girlfriend appears like a nymph, transparent, draped in air and her long blond locks. Her feet are small, lovely, with scarlet toenails; a thin golden chain coils around her ankle.

As soon as she steps into the room, she's enveloped in sunlight, and I tremble to touch her, such slim shoulders and perfect breasts. She doesn't protest but guides my hands farther along her thighs; her skin mellows under my fingers. She has a shaved pussy, red and tender like her mouth. It opens and closes—a wet, living thing. I come inside her, she arches, buttocks raised, heels pounding at my back when she calls out my brother's name.

"Happy fucking graduation," Konstantin says and grins. In the doorway, his naked erect silhouette looms too far and too close.

❉ ❉ ❉

Since high school, I'd dreamed of becoming a radiologist; I was convinced it was the best profession in the world because you were able to see the invisible, to see inside people. But I couldn't afford medical school, or my own apartment, and I couldn't bring myself to ask Konstantin for help because it would've meant that I'd conceded to his despicable behavior, endorsed his impudence. I never could have done that, stooping so low, humiliating myself to no end. So I worked long hours at the kiosk, every day and even on weekends, saving what little I could. My mother, however, had lost her job three years into *perestroika* when it had become clear that only the young and the dodgy would lead Russia into the 21st century. Konstantin was one of them; he possessed no degree but plenty of talent, criminal talent. He had the nose of a bloodhound, he smelled money and fortune, and he chased them to the death. He believed in the imminent success of his clandestine undertakings as other people believed in their government that kept robbing them of chance and hope, a desire to achieve. Konstantin often said that socialism was about petty theft; *perestroika* was about grand larceny. One must adjust, and one must share. Years later, reading about ordered killings that would slowly become routine, I understood that "sharing" had always been unwarranted and through sheer coercion. It was a continuous game of Russian roulette — each lucky, missed shot brought you closer to death.

Little Konstantin had moved into Big Konstantin's apartment and my mother's heart with ease and confidence, without doing much of anything other than curling on her lap and eating her food — beef cutlets, *rassol'nik*, fried fish. Just like Big Konstantin, he exuded restlessness and was a voracious eater, yet remained skinny. Each time my mother picked him up, she worried about breaking him in half. He was almost five but looked barely three. He was inquisitive and intrusive, and I compared him to a rescue pet too eager to trust any feeding hand. Unlike me, my mother had never questioned Konstantin's paternity and embraced the boy with the kind of selfless love only a grandmother could bestow. And Little Konstantin indulged her, melting under her stroking hands like snow under the sun. He laughed when she bathed him, tickling his feet, and nestled with her on the couch, watching cartoons or an old TV show, *In the World of Animals*. Each day they went out for walks and returned with sweets and toys. They built Lego castles and race tracks, improvised a puppet theater from old gloves, and held imaginary tournaments, transforming themselves into great warriors, fierce and fearless, protected by cardboard armor. My mother turned twenty-five again, with a life marked by promise and a kid's touch. She gained weight, grew breasts, and colored her hair chestnut brown; she wore young women's clothes, tight and uncomfortable, but also low-cut and low-rise, hems dragging across the floor. Even her face filled in and blossomed, a touch of rosy glow on her cheeks. In just a week, Little Konstantin was calling her Big Mama.

"Konstantin means constant, everlasting," my mother said once, during supper. She reached to touch the boy's head, his pixie face softened by long brown locks.

"And Leova?" he asked.

"Bold for his people. Lion," she answered.

"King," I said.

"You don't look like a king. You're too short."

"Sorry." I spooned dressed herring into my mouth, chewing steadily.

"If you have a son," he continued, "will you call him Little Leova or Lion Prince?"

"You think you're so fucking smart."

"You think you're so fucking smart."

"Stop it. Both of you," my mother said.

Little Konstantin focused his soft, woolly eyes on my face; I glanced out the window, at a large icicle that hung low over the sill, threatening to crush against its silver lip.

❊ ❊ ❊

The year is 1995. It's our mother's 50th birthday, and Konstantin has ordered 50 burgundy roses to be delivered to our old flat. A stylist has been hired to pick out our mother's dress and massive chest-crushing jewelry, a calf-hair purse and a matching pair of high-heeled shoes our mother has trouble wearing. She wobbles from the bathroom to the kitchen to the living room, pausing and ogling herself in a dim hallway mirror. A driver in a black Mercedes has been paid to chaperone her to a spa that morning, where she's been transformed into someone with a pompadour and flawless skin.

An Italian restaurant has been reserved months in advance, friends gathered, wines selected and paired with exotic seafood platters and hand-rolled pastas in rich blood-red sauces. In the background a band is playing "Yesterday," and the guy impersonating Lennon shakes his long, stringy hair. Waitresses hover over the table, where our tall, rejuvenated mother presides between her sons. Konstantin pricks a shrimp and spools a forkful of pasta, raises a wine glass. "If you wanted to punish a bad person, what would you do, Ma?" he asks, sucking the pasta off the fork, chewing with applied force.

"Me?" she asks, confused.

"Yes." He dabs a napkin at his lips. "Would you kill him? Or would you make him suffer for the rest of his life?"

"Whose life? Who are you talking about? No one deserves to die," she says, the confusion in her eyes having given way to fear. She blinks and rubs her cheek, her glowing complexion now smudged between her fingers.

"You're too kind, Ma. Always have been—to all of us assholes," he says and downs the wine, beckoning the waitress, who obliges at once, a bottle of red in hand.

"Speak for yourself," I say. "And stop interrogating our mother, you heartless jerk."

"You heartless jerk. What did you ever do to care for her? What did you give her? I paid for everything, including your fucking suit."

"Money is paper."

"Money is freedom—freedom to do whatever I damn well please."

"Steal and murder?"

"Wow, some potent words, little brother. Be careful, someone may hear you."

"Mom, is that true?" I turn sideways. "Did he buy my suit? You said it was your money, and I said I'd pay you back."

She squints, hard, as though one of us were about to hit her. "Why do you always have to do this?" she grinds the words between her teeth like dry buckwheat. "Spoil everything?"

"I spoil everything? I'm the culprit of all your troubles?" My voice escalates; my stomach churns with anger. A few guests snap their heads in our direction. "I'll sing," I say and acknowledge the empty stage, the instruments, like dead bodies, scattered on the floor. "It's my gift to all of you." I get up, the wine pulsing through my veins. My mother catches my hand, tries to hold me in place.

"Don't embarrass yourself, asshole," Konstantin smirks.

"Can you pay me *not* to?"

❈   ❈   ❈

When, even before the funeral, the police asked my mother whether she was aware of the criminal activities her older son had been involved in, she shook her head and said, "It's your job to know such things and prevent them from happening. My job is to love and protect my children. And sometimes we all fail."

Oddly, I began feeling like that too. There was sad helplessness in everything I did, an unnerving importunate sense of paralysis, an inability to derive satisfaction from food or studies or even sex, however sporadic—I wasn't in a relationship. I didn't love anyone and no one loved me. I had money but no one special to spend it on; I lived in a beautiful apartment but couldn't wait to escape in the morning. Even worse, I no longer desired to become a radiologist. I had lost all interest, all ambition to see inside people.

They seemed no more than a compilation of organs damaged by age or disease. They feared death and accidents, the unavoidable and the unknown. There was no cure for them and no hope.

It was early spring in the city, the roads a marsh of snow and dirt. Wet, murky air clung to faces, coated buildings and trees. The river had begun to thaw and you could see a plexus of cracks sprawling out toward a dark spot in the middle, barely scabbed with ice. We still hadn't heard anything from Little Konstantin's mother, and by the time the big icicle broke off and crushed against the kitchen sill, he had stopped leaping from chairs or scampering to answer the phone. Occasionally, though, I would spot him by the window, quiet but tense, his baby palms pressed against the cold, foggy glass. He would stand like that for a while, unperturbed by voices or house noise, a bug frozen in time.

"He's gone," my mother said as soon as I arrived from work one day. She stood by the kitchen window, her coat bunched at her feet. I could tell she'd been crying, her face blotched red, her hair adhered to puffy cheeks.

"What do you mean? His mother returned?"

She shook her head. "They took him."

"Who took him? What the fuck happened?"

"We were rolling snow, what's left of it. We had to move quickly to cover a larger territory. A taxi pulled over. I turned around and he was gone." She sobbed into my sweater, and I lifted my arms around her.

"We have to get him back," she said and wiped her face with the stretched sleeve. "We have to pay ransom. They called. Konstantin owed a hundred thousand."

"Dollars? No fucking way."

"I can't let them take my baby."

"We go to the police."

"They're all corrupt. And what will we say? That Little Konstantin's mother left him? We have no proof. He'll be placed in a home. I can't let that happen. He's mine."

"But he isn't. Don't you see?"

"No." Her forehead strained in protest. "I love him. He belongs with me."

"What if he doesn't?"

"Don't say that."

"What if the trick is not to love someone so much that he doesn't disappear or run away?"

She stared at me. "Are you making a joke? Because it isn't funny. I've loved you equally, but he was the one who needed me more. Can't you understand that?"

"No. Because in the end, it didn't save him but made him do crazy, ugly things. So he could be the man our father wasn't. So he could send you on posh vacations, buy you fancy clothes, this apartment—" She slapped me, her hand just as quick and hard as eighteen years ago when I'd told her that I nearly drowned and Konstantin was responsible.

For the next two days we didn't leave the apartment and we didn't talk, passing a few cautious words like explosives, with nervous fear. On the third day, clouds blew over the city, gray like rocks, and it began to rain. The river darkened and swelled and began moving. Large, jagged floes drifted along the snow-fringed banks. Out the window, the floes resembled wrecked ships or parts of buildings with the remnants of life stuck to their broken surfaces. We waited by the phone. We knew we didn't have that much money in Konstantin's account, and selling either apartment, old or new, would take time, but perhaps we could negotiate about transferring the property over to the kidnappers.

The caller turned out to be an older woman with a scratchy voice who coughed short, incomplete sentences into the receiver: Bring the money. Leave the money. Pick up the kid. No police or the kid dies. Her words penetrated the distance and my ear in quick forced jabs.

"Let me talk to the boy," I said as soon as she stopped. "I want to make sure he's alive."

I heard a few muffled sounds as though someone were wrestling with the phone or conferring in a hurry. I switched to the speaker so my mother could hear the entire conversation, her pale face a tempest of emotions.

"Hello," I said, then louder, "Hello?"

"Big Mama," Little Konstantin said.

"I'm here," she answered. "I'm here, baby."

"Big Papa is—"and the line went dead, an echo of empty beeps spreading through the kitchen.

My mother stared at the phone, then at me, her eyes wet like river pebbles.

"That motherfucker," I said, spitting. "That goddamned motherfucker."

The cab driver had no problem finding the neighborhood of shabby, piss-reeking five-story buildings—*khrushchevki*—about to be demolished like the rest. In the yard, as I got out of the taxi, I spotted a filthy tailless dog scrabbling about a pile of trash. He pulled out a chicken leg, scraps of skin on a dry bone, and began gnawing. I stood watching him, but for just a moment, a heresy of rain and snow in my eyes.

I ran up the steps, found the door, rang the bell. I pounded and threatened until I heard a sly shuffle, the chain being lifted, the bolt turned, the sound a wall clock makes when it's about to strike an hour. As a boy, I must've imagined our meeting many times, only in reverse—I was the one standing behind the door, waiting to embrace the visitor, hoping him to be my father. I never imagined his face but thought of him as a healthy tree, with a thick trunk, shapely outreaching limbs, lush brown hair rustling in the wind. When the door cracked open and was pulled back by an invisible someone, I found myself facing a short middle-aged woman with yellowish skin and frightened eyes. She was like a bird plucked of all feathers, thin, humble, about to die.

"Where is he?" I asked, and she pointed along the dark narrow corridor, where amidst the junk shelves and coats I detected something moving, slinking along the wall. It was a man in a wheelchair, Little Konstantin on his lap.

"Lion King! Lion King!" The boy jumped off, scurrying in my direction. I bent down and picked him up. He was warm, soft, and smelled of baked apples. A streak of white had crusted on his cheek. He was dressed in the same blue mohair sweater and jeans as the day he'd disappeared, but the clothes seemed to have been washed, the jeans ironed. "Big Papa said you were coming to get me."

"Oh, yeah? What else did Big Papa say? That he is a thief and liar? A goddamned motherfucking asshole?"

"Stop cussing in my home," the man in the wheelchair said. He was almost bald, with a cleft in his prickly jaw. His nose was crooked and his small eyes too close together, wincing at the light the woman switched on. He was dressed in a plaid flannel shirt and gray sweatpants stretched at the ankles; he made me think of street beggars, those fetid bums in train stations and subways. I felt no pity toward him and, sadly, no anger.

"I'm Liya, Boris's wife," the woman said, and I recognized

her voice, so weak and raspy, as though an animal had been clawing at her throat. She handed me the little coat and boots. "We're very sorry. Please, forgive us."

I didn't answer.

"Make a scary face and snarl at them," Little Konstantin said. "Like when you study for your exams and I want to play."

I patted his head, then sat him down and began threading his arms through the coat sleeves.

"Fucking assholes," I finally said. "How could you?"

My father wheeled closer, his feet in green corduroy slippers touching my shins. "He did this to me."

"Shut the fuck up," I said. "You don't get to blame him."

"Konstantin wanted me to go back to your mother. Offered me money and a new apartment. When I said no, those punks forced me to lie on the ground while he drove his car across my legs. She was there," he pointed at Liya, who nodded, fighting tears.

"So you stole his child? That's your piss-ass excuse? The fuck is wrong with you?"

"I need surgery. Abroad. I may be able to walk with prosthetics."

"Did you pay someone to kill Konstantin?"

He shook his head, vigorously. "No, no. I'm not like that."

"How would I know?"

"You're my son."

"Fuck off."

"I sent money, when I could."

"What's my name?"

He didn't answer but cupped his knees; the woman leaned over and whispered something in his ear.

I held Little Konstantin's hand as we sauntered out of the apartment.

"I bet she didn't love you like that," my father yelled. "Did she? Did she?"

I stalled, reached into my pocket and pulled out money, all I had. "Here," I said, turning and foisting a hefty stack into Liya's hand. "Don't buy him new legs, though. He might walk away." I laughed, a dry, choked laugh, the kind I imagined Konstantin laughed when the gun fired but before the bullet made it all dark and irrevocable.

❊ ❊ ❊

It's summer already. I got accepted into medical school and am veering toward cardiology, the science of the heart. Konstantin has been drawing and cutting them out of paper, so that hearts of various sizes and colors are scattered about the apartment—red, purple, deep orange, the color of the bloody sun pulsing over the city. The Moskva River rushes, meanders along the grassy banks. Every now and then, large boats sail by, the water parts and closes, the circles diminish and finally disappear, one inside another.

It has taken a thick yellow envelope three weeks to travel from America to Russia, and I don't show it to my mother at first. But when I do, she cries silently, hot tears streaming down her cheeks, falling into the *pelmeni* dough. She continues to roll it out thin, thinner than skin or hair. "We can still visit," she says. "Can't we? The mother won't mind. How hard is it to get a visa?" I shrug and take her warm, sticky hands in mine, and she holds on to my thumbs like a child, with all her might.

The next day, Konstantin and I are dressed in shorts and old-fashioned *matroskas*, cotton sailors' shirts our mother bought at the market. We look ridiculous but are hesitant to shed a smile or a word, standing low on the riverbank so that our toes touch its wet lip. An armada of birds flies into the trees hooded with foliage. The limbs bounce and sway and finally settle, the birds concealed among the leaves.

In his hand, Konstantin holds a toy lion he arranges inside a warped black-leather shoe I found in the yard, when all the snow had melted.

"He won't drown?" he asks. "Will he?"

I blink. "No. Of course not."

"Are there lions in America?"

"Yes. Everywhere. Big lions, with thick manes and sharp teeth." I shake my head and snarl at him; he lets out a shy giggle and leaps backward. We are silent, but just for a moment, observing a tremble of clouds on the water.

We lower the shoe into the river and push it downstream with a severed tree branch. We watch the shoe sail, reluctant at first, bobbing on waves and leaning to one side. When it disappears from view, we climb up the bank and continue to watch it drift, straight ahead, unimpeded—oblivious to anything but water and wind.

What the Neighbors Know

What the neighbors know is so small it might fit in my mailbox.
I wish they would put it there, unfolded, explicit, so I could be
certain of what they think they saw, the shaky black-and-white
reel they have colorized, the beginnings and middles cobbled
to find their way to the end.

No one will sign his name. Each separate letter will be cut
from newspapers, magazines, to keep the scales of knowing
unbalanced: *We have a piece of your life that we plan to torture
into something we recognize. We want more pieces. But
even then, we won't give you this one back.*

I once had all of their names, but didn't keep them. Did they
keep mine? If we passed each other in some far-off town,
I wouldn't know them, though I have lived beside them
for nearly thirty years. Anonymity is a chosen loneliness,
but a secret in a cul-de-sac has a fleeting life.

Their eyes on my comings and goings, my middling tragedy,
are a kind of extortion, even if they never open their mouths.
If I do not give them reasons, they will think I had none.
If enough people paint me a heart of pitch, a rudderless
integrity, how could all of them be wrong?

Whatever the neighbors know, it is not enough, but the rest
of the story is not mine to tell. See me, then, half in shadow. Or
turn me, if you must, toward your lurid light. I will grow older,
quieter, until no one believes the tale you pin on me. I will wear
sensible shoes. I will outfox you by being too dull to be bad.

In a Handbasket

River cane would make a snug ride, or maybe
the black rushes of a Gullah sweetgrass,
but if I am going (and it seems as though

I might), I'd like to choose my own conveyance.
Pine needle or willow, cattail or bamboo—
(if I went in a basket of bamboo, I could soothe

myself by chanting, softly, *Bamboo, bamboo,
bamboo,* for surely hell would seem
less sinister with that charm of b's on

my tongue). I thought at first, no matter
the method—whether coiled or twined, woven
or plaited—but it seems now that coils

would be a coward's way. Too easy
to burrow down and not look out on mayhem.
Better the burden of a weave with holes

for peering through—a wicker transport.
Certainly not the blindfold offered by those
Nantucket baskets with their scrimshawed lids;

I won't go quaking in shadow beneath a pretty
cover of etched ivory or bone. I should know
where I am going. Color is incidental. No need

for the stark white and black the Hopis wove
from sun-bleached yucca, the dark seed pods
of Devil's Claw. No pigments, dyes or paints,

for I prefer the earth tones of Indonesian vines,
or the bulrush grasses of the low country.
If I need a comfort on my way, give me

that scent of rattan that wafts from every
emporium of the Far East, or the clean balm
that lingers where dunes bar the sea.

Let this final going be the one act in my life
to which I give ample and deliberate thought.
Let me dally a long time, choosing.

Manly Johnson, photograph

Touch

I grow old today like the unused garage door swollen stuck
in summer. This is our atonement for beauty. It is

proportional, sorrow, how the jays call to us with the blue
flash of their bodies near where my wife used to garden.

We take our flesh and make of it one hundred drums,
the erasure of the body's mud.

And if I tell myself I prepare for death in the soapy smell of my
hands as I dry them with a towel, I dream the rain dyes the grass

a darker green, staining it with a congress of touch, making of it art
that later, evaporating without fanfare, returns to air—

with the same ease that come January
this door will fall back open to my hand.

Moon Letters

When she sees her older boy throwing stones
into the river, she imagines the moon after dark

floating with a certain buoyancy above her,
the grass outside the windows covering the open

mouth of yard. Every field at first light becomes
an elegy: insects lifting from the swales,

clouds thin as starving horses, the mud of
the river weaving through the milkweed and sumac.

And she carries the strata of the years like an ache
each time she thinks of the younger boy she lost

in her sixth month, her belly for so long afterwards
a ghostly blossoming. And she watches after dark

how the moon whitewashes sorrow, lacquering
the shadows on the grass. We come to this out of our

bodies, she knows, a breath of clouds drifting
slowly overhead, ripe with rain that cannot bring

itself to fall, the hours sifting like embalming fluid
through our limbs, burrowing inside bones that are

hollowed out, tunneled with grief, black flowers
in night's garden. Then morning arrives once more,

annotated by birdcalls. There is a grackle with
dark eyes, a shapelessness of wind across

the field, each hour conjuring primitive
voices, the sun performing her morning

ablutions. These are our bodies and our smoke,
our sprung notes becoming emptiness,

the years as lonely as a tuft of a weed.

Nine Crows

There were nine crows in nine days
watching from the shadows of the trees.

Black birds with black eyes, their folding
shrouds of wings thrashing blind

and corrosive—shadow stains—the creatures
cawing like breaking glass. Death was

the papery hive on the back porch, a maple
broken at its back, a rumor of stars and a catechism

of snake and sky. Later there was a skin of dust
on the window sill, a cellar lined with Mason

jars—something listing milky and mysterious inside.
And always the crow woman across the road

with her salves of celadine and musk flowers,
a thick green muck congealing atop the creek,

crabapples falling then decaying—dream fruit
blossoming into crows and foulmouthed

spells, the birds climbing into the amniotic light
toward a dilated moon roseate and clothed

in mist across the open sore of sky.

Crow Sight

When my uncle was going blind, hunters were uncertain shapes
beyond the trees, even with orange vests. He believed, then,

in the uncertainty of things, the hours clinging like smoke,
the years a kind of inwardness. What was knowable, it seemed,

was the moon with its small enclave of fever, indistinct in
the night sky. Come August hoot owls called out in strange

metrical forms, and a dense heat left salt crystallizing on his skin,
a cuneiform writing. In one dream there was no discernible pattern

to the world, and he imagined he saw a coyote wandering out
of a great fire, appearing like a coal miner emerging from a cave's

mouth, singed black and drunk on smoke, staggering,
head down, coming toward him out of the slow heat of day.

Months later, in a light snow, he watched a lone man walking in
the field, wearing a bright stocking cap, carrying across his shoulders

a small buck, the head and meager branches of horns lolling,
the four legs drooping forward, the white of the belly curling

around the neck. My uncle insisted this was his final memory
of sight: a few drops of blood—what a dog in heat might

leave—dotting the trail of snow along the fence.

Geraniums

—for Henry 1938 - 2010

I wanted to tell you to photograph
the blond woman who leaned
out the upstairs window next door
to water geraniums in a windowbox.

She wore a blue blouse
the geraniums were pink.
Or she wore a pink blouse
the flowers were blue. Or
she wore no blouse her nipples
were pink and her eyes were blue.
Her hair gathered loosely up
by a flowered scarf.

You faced me and could not
have seen what I saw—
a woman smiling over some flowers,
her hair, her blouse, her bare arm
honeyed with sun;
she was bending toward you
with her watering can.

You were losing your eyes;
I wanted to give you the gift
of this photograph. Maybe
you could paint it yet, the way
Vuillard would have done,
on a scrap of cardboard,
her blouse, the loosened hair
luminous in the forever afternoon.

Maybe you knew her name —
someone who comes to the shore
every year. Maybe
a guest of the neighbors,
though she leaned from the window
and watered those flowers
as if they were her own.

In the old days we could have
watched for her to go out of the house
and down to the beach with her towel.
We could have followed, pretending
to wade nearby where she could see us,
could feel like sun on her skin
our unabashed admiration.

And later we might have found
some excuse for knocking at her door,
for presenting our hearts to be broken.

Kimberly Colantino, "Evening Shadows," photograph

The Oat Bitch & the Old Man's Daughters

It's an old story
and I suffered it.
How the patriarch fell
and the tractor fell silent.

How wind stirred
among the crowd of oat sheaves
left standing in the field

as if his spirit
waited among them.

How a stranger came
in the guise of a preacher
to lift, unwitting, the last
sheaf to the wagon.

Who bent his head to the load
in prayer or resignation.

How the sheaf-goat
dressed as a child
lifted a pitchfork to stick it
into the wagonload
as the tractor leapt ahead.

How the stranger,
as in a ritual of harvest,
came to be killed.

I was that stranger. I
bled to the tines'
victorious singing. Bled
for the Oat Bitch's hunger.

They laid me down
by the howling thresher,
torn half-naked
and shorn of disguise.

Cleansed and poulticed
my body with unguents
so I no longer knew myself
or how long I died

but awoke one day to silence
and the curious balm
conferred on my wounds
by the old man's daughters.

Mark Weiss, photograph

Bane

I thought I had another year to kiss
the Doll's Eye Bane, and call
the Saw-whet Owl out of the dark.

I had it from Gerald Stern, who taught me
how to be a Jew, and not those know-it-alls
down at the Campus Snack, calling out
"Nurse" when they wanted beer
and hoo-hooing after her thunder thighs.

I thought I had another year to sow
a batch of slippery newbies in the pond,
to watch the mink slip under the ice
and harvest a crop of golden carp
on a sighing day in sweet October.

I had it from Lame Deer, who showed me
how to be an Indian, with his fable about
the Great Spirit and the Chicken,
though there was the problem of Grandmother
in her doeskin wedding dress and quill beads.

And how I learned to talk again after years
of building haystacks by the creek, one line
of a poem cut into the grease and chaff
of the gearshift housing, and arriving over
and over with clenched teeth and only that to say.

I thought I had another year to kiss
the Doll's Eye Bane, and call my cousins,
the Saw-whet and the Barred and the Great Horned Owl
out of the dark and, for those few minutes
of coded conversation, not be afraid.

Weights and Measures

In the New Year we imagine
the snow begins to sing.
Also the mud. We remember
the sadness caught in its throat.

There was war when I walked
to kindergarten, and I was afraid
of shadows as I went through the woods.
The little rug I had to borrow
at naptime had sadness in it.

How many times
have I slept through the birth
of the seventeen-year locusts?
How many lovers have slept beside me,
waiting to leave in the morning?

Because we are older now,
someone will ask us to lead the way.
We will try to recall a story
with a lesson in it.

Grace Dissolving Barriers

That summer was my first experience
with the seventeen-year locusts. They crawled out
from everywhere—hatching, my father said,
from holes in the trees after a long dormancy,
assaulting us with their grotesque greenish-black
bodies—red eyes bulging, wings buzzing loudly—
an army that's come to conquer and occupy.

And then, the sickening sweet scent all summer long
of bodies rotting, or maybe it was the odor of the light
brown shells they left behind, the color of pork rinds.
Our bike tires crunched endlessly over them—
hundreds of thousands piled high against
the curbs and fence posts, scattered into gutters.
There was no escaping them.

I had never been so disgusted with death
since the time my parents dragged me to
Wapner's Funeral Parlor to view Great-Uncle Charlie
when I was six—the hushed voices of adults
in dark suits and dresses, Great-Aunt Mildred draped
in her ever-present mink, its mean little face
snapped tight to its tail and that strange sweet scent
of drooping flowers, or was it the waxy husk lying
in its narrow bed, hands folded, fingernails so clean
—not a speck of dirt anywhere.

The summer of the locusts I was fourteen—the last
season of bicycles for a long while, the summer I read
everything I could about the Holocaust, names of death
camps ringing in my ears—Treblinka, Auschwitz, Dachau.
I even brought along *Anguish of the Jews* on vacation,

reading in the car all the way to Virginia Beach
scrunched between my father and uncle in the front seat,
adrift in this latest revelation of humanity, its chronicle
of cruelty. What possessed me?
It couldn't have been the locusts and yet —
all those burnt husks, the sheer number of the Dead.

Shoshana Kertesz, "Old Graveyard," photograph

FINALIST
C. WHITE

Dominion

I found her on the porch,
breast up, wings outstretched.
A Cooper's Hawk,
genius of stealth and speed.
She must have been doing sixty
when my window broke her neck.
I cursed the glass.
I cursed suburbia, and fate,
though I don't really believe
in fate. And yet, hadn't she died
on my doorstep? Was I meant
somehow to claim her?
I wrapped her in an old t-shirt,
took a shovel from the shed
and began to dig,
considering, not the world
she'd lost —
forest, flight, mate —
but how best to render
the tapering feathers
barred with black, the talons
like yellow needles.

Communion

I envy crows their looks —
sitting shiva on power lines,
or massed in raucous wheat field wakes —
they seem cut out for grief.
If I were death's omen,
Poe's badass bird of woe,
I'd visit you more often, stay longer.
I'd drive the wrens and pompous robins
from your grave, then feast
on the life that feasts on you.

Eleanor Leonne Bennett, "Feather on Bone," photograph

Hungry Lake

In those days I buried dead animals,
wrapping them in sumac leaves
and tying their wilted bodies
with thick blades of crabgrass.

Mid-winter, when the ground was frozen
I would roll birch bark around the body,
loop in a cherry stem for a button and push
my hand with the dead into the snow.

Animals die here every year.
The locals say the lake is hungry,
that in order to survive a blizzard
a man will cut open his entire herd

one by one and move barefoot in snow
stepping naked from cow to cow until
the good weather returns. Imagine when
snow melts, the village of carcasses unearthed.

Clean bones from those winter burials rise
and find their way here. I paint these bones
over and over. There are acres
of memorial mounds posing in the fields.

Sometimes a bit of blue from the lake
laps in, then ice thickens or birds
ascend then disappear into clouds
or night comes and a full moon rises.

In the dark I hear a loon calling
from across the lake. She is hungry
for her mate. I grip my brush hard
ready to dip into the depth of color

to touch this blank canvas of snow.
I answer the loon in the voice
of a star dying. When the snow falls
I paint them, all these naked bones.

Shoshana Kertesz, "Lake II," photograph

Wildfire

He started the fire, but no flames took hold.
Heat ate all the oxygen that last night
of his month-long disappearance.

Had I found him then,
opening the door to the cabin
would have caused an explosion,
could have killed someone.

Opening the door, days after he died,
soot stirred and settled again.

Bananas were baked on the counter,
too black for bread, everything
was melted off the walls.

No time visible on the clock,
La Persistencia de la Memoria destroyed.

He started the fire *here*,
with his lips on mine,
blowing air in me as if through an oboe reed.
He blew so much air into me

flames took hold. He pounded my chest
as if it were a tympani and awoke a burning field,
my Norwegian grandmothers chanting,

å spise, drikke på ditt ord.
Oh, he ate and drank me
like that field on fire.

The neighbors running with buckets,
with wet rags, anything to contain it.

Nothing contains me now,
untying these tight knots
on the bags from the funeral home,
stretching out my soot covered hands.

Oh, this burning field expands
the picture, goes past the frame,

is frameless. This field of flames
burns our lying down together and rising up,
burns the house, the barn, the cattle,

burns these words and this song,
the rooster crowing another dawn.

In Drought, in Rain

Out buying your birthday gift I run into a friend, new
in love. He hasn't slept in days, the thought of the woman
wound so tightly around his chest he can barely breathe.

I am just buying you a book. I tell you this over dinner.
We eat, remember storms in the desert, when every surface
glowed with the electricity of the sky—dusty wind across the bed,

the morning wet and polished. Now the cat sleeps on our quiet bed,
her paws across the pillows. Our breathing is steady, patient. But here:
my arms reach over you like a tree bough, the light on the mountains.

No, I come to you in the morning as if you were a wheat field,
an orchard, and I am a bird who has been hungry all night.

Tracey Harris, "You Don't Have To Be Perfect,"
oil on board, 14" x 11"

My Father's Fastball

Sometimes I like to imagine the other end
of one of my father's pitches—

not the backyard base-running of my childhood,
but the pitches when he was younger,

his four-seamer or slider, speed that would sting
when the ball hit your glove. Age 42, the fair's

pitching booth clocked him at 88;
he won a Pepsi t-shirt to prove it.

When I was older I learned about the contract
with the Pirates: the *no playing on Sunday* boy from Calvin College

turned it down. Went on to be a preacher,
coach; did pretty okay on the local teams.

I've always known my father with a scar on his knee.
When my husband turned 30, my father

mourned the passing as his own, said he'd known
he would never pitch that fast again.

It was all downhill from there.
The real prize at the fair was out-pitching

the younger guys. With his fastball at the top
of the carnie's chalkboard, my sister and I

had new teddy bears while our father—
for a night—remembered the mound,

the wind-up, the release when the ball left his hand.

The Elephants

Three elephants strung trunk
to tail in red and violent robes lumbered
the way down behind the hearse
into high noon. All the day's
gray rain pooled
on their swaying backs, as one
tear tracks another, then
joins it. And so
we buried you, emptied of
the last small waters
of your life.

With you I entombed *father*,
the tether of *offspring*,
filibuster, soliloquy,
asides to the audience, coda,
prelude, notebooks stuffed
with stallings for time,
sleepwalkings, caught breaths, foxhole prayers,
the mechanical whirr and sweep
of the searchlight across your
dry sea, light hover,
gravitas.

Your grave mounds, duned
by skittish winds.
The clang of mourning bells
against tough hides joins
the other silence. The sand
eddies up and descends,
the way a cyclone in a hooded
night picks out one tiny sleeping
head in its attic bed
and funnels up
the child.

Paracosmos

Leslie traced their difficulties to before the parrot fever scare, to before even the chimney sweep's scrotum, to the summer night when her husband proposed naming the baby Quarantina. "She'll be Tina, for short," said Hugh, who'd recently been appointed public health officer for the county, and only then did Leslie realize he wasn't joking. Other names on his list included Hygienia, Inoculata, and Malaria. "Doesn't Malaria Malansky have a ring to it?" he asked. "She'd be a constant reminder of the work that's yet to be done in the Third World." Leslie preferred Victoria or Elizabeth. In the end, they'd settled upon Eve—after Madame Curie's daughter—but not before the man who was supposed to understand her completely had referred to their future child as a "missed opportunity." So she shouldn't have been terribly shocked, nine years later, when Hugh's intransigence made Evie the pariah of Mrs. Driscoll's fourth-grade classroom.

Evie's best friend that autumn was a chatty, shameless redhead named Kim Pitchford who lived two doors away, and hardly an afternoon passed without that relentless tyke jabbering up a typhoon in their living room. But at lunch one overcast Sunday, Kim informed Evie—and Hugh—that carrying an umbrella increased the likelihood of rain. This roused the scientific lion in Leslie's husband. Hugh promptly delivered an extemporaneous sermon on cause and effect, which began with the unfortunate remark, "Take the scrotum of the chimney sweep," and led to a tale of how some long-dead English surgeon had deduced the relationship between soot and genital tumors. Leslie returned from her tennis match to hear Evie asking, "Papa, what's a chimney sweep?" It wasn't until three hours later that Rebecca Pitchford phoned to demand an explanation.

"You have to apologize and promise her it won't happen again," Leslie warned her husband. "What were you thinking? *Were* you thinking?"

"I'm not going to censor myself for some airhead," snapped Hugh. "Men have scrotums. Men die of cancer. That's reality—and nine years old is more than old enough for some basic reality. If I'm going to call Rebecca about anything, it's about all that standing water on their property. To mosquitoes carrying West Nile virus, each of those birdbaths looks like a five-course meal."

And so the conflict with Kim's parents spiraled out of control. Rebecca Pitchford wouldn't be squaring the circle anytime soon—there was no arguing with Hugh about that—but she did have a vengeful streak, and two weeks later, Evie was the only fourth-grader in Hager Hills not invited to Kim's tenth birthday party. In fact, the redhead dropped Evie cold, carrying with her their daughter's other friends, until one afternoon Leslie's beauty came off the school bus sobbing, "Nobody loves me anymore."

"*I* love you," cried Leslie, hugging the child to her chest. "*Papa* loves you." And to console the girl, she promised the only gift Evie wanted even more than the companionship of her peers: a talking parakeet.

Ever since they'd visited the aviary at the Bronx Zoo, Evie had been pleading for a conversational bird. The girl could draw colorful mynahs and cockatiels as though conjured from her imagination, then label each species with precision. She knew both English and Latin names from memory. Even Leslie's personal distaste for birds—their odor, their racket—proved no match for the tears of her rejected child.

"I hope you're not going to be upset," she implored Hugh in bed that night. "It was killing me, seeing her like that. . . . So I agreed we'd get her a parakeet."

"Not in ten million years," said Hugh. "Are you insane?"

"I know it's going to be a hassle—"

"A hassle? It's a *hazard*. Jesus, Leslie. We're in the middle of a silent psittacosis epidemic." Hugh's eyes locked on hers. "Parrot fever. Ornithosis. Two years ago, a petshop owner died right down the turnpike in New Brunswick. Do you really want to expose Evie to pneumonia—to the risk of meningitis?"

"But plenty of people own parakeets," pleaded Leslie.

"Plenty of people also smoke cigarettes and eat raw shellfish and ride motorcycles without helmets. Evie isn't plenty of people." Hugh caressed her bare shoulder. "Look, I'm sorry. If I'd known Rebecca would be such a bitch, I'd have swallowed my pride."

"You still could . . ."

"I already phoned her from the office. She wasn't interested."

So the next evening, they sat down together with Evie in her intensely pink bedroom and explained why she couldn't have a parakeet. To Leslie's surprise, their daughter merely shrugged off the disappointment. "Lauren brought her macaw for our sleepover," said Evie. "And her macaw knows five thousand words."

Leslie exchanged a nervous glance with her husband. "Lauren?" she asked.

"My *new* best friend," said Evie. Then she turned to a patch of vacant air between the halogen floor lamp and the colossal stuffed leopard that her uncle had won for her at a carnival, and she ordered Lauren, "Tell your macaw to say something."

After a splash of silence, Evie bubbled with laughter.

"See," said their daughter between giggles. "Isn't she great?"

Leslie looked to Hugh for guidance, but he was staring at the empty space, wearing an expression of bewilderment. With each passing second of laughter, she felt Evie drifting further from her toward a world of imaginary birds.

"What did Lauren's macaw say, princess?" she finally asked.

Her daughter's laughter faded rapidly into a sullen pout.

"Come on, Mommy. You have to listen carefully."

In the foyer ten minutes later, Leslie found her entire body trembling. "I'm scared, Hugh. She's too old for imaginary friends."

"It's a phase. It's perfectly healthy," Hugh reassured her. "Let's just hope that Lauren's mother is less of a bitch than Kim's."

❊ ❊ ❊

Sally Whiskers had been Leslie's invisible companion for a brief spell during her own childhood: a chimeric creature, part-human and part-feline, who fulfilled Leslie's desires for both a best friend and a house cat. They'd hunted mice together in kindergarten—much to the alarm of the school psychologist. But in first grade, her twin brother asserted that he was also friends with Sally, and Leslie still remembered the car ride when she contended he was lying, that he *couldn't* be friends with Sally, because Sally was imaginary. And that had been that. Hugh, she was amused and delighted to discover, had also once befriended a daydream. Doctor Charley Horse. Her husband had even demanded that his father buy the make-believe physician a plastic stethoscope of his own. But if Evie had inherited a proclivity for fantasy from both of her parents, Leslie sensed at the outset that "Lauren Dowdy" was different: more complex, more demanding, *more real.*

While chatty Kim Pitchford had been a daily visitor to their home, voiceless Lauren practically moved in. She joined them for supper every evening, and Evie insisted that a place setting be laid for her at the kitchen table. Some mornings, the child slept over and stayed for breakfast—and Evie insisted on filling a second bowl of cereal, then discarding it when Lauren didn't eat on account of a "tummy ache." The imaginary girl required her own toothbrush, her own jack-o-lantern at Halloween, her own turn when Evie's grandfather bestowed piggyback rides. Leslie's brother took Evie and his three daughters to the grand opening of Adventure America, an indoor amusement park in Atlantic City, and he had to negotiate a separate seat for the invisible girl on the carousel. Evie's new playmate boasted a rich and uncannily consistent history that set her apart from the run-of-the-mill pretend friends that Leslie read about during her Internet research. She had a birthday, a scar on her right knee from a water-skiing mishap, even a nickel allergy. Like Kim, she enjoyed fiery red hair and chalk-pale skin. On a whim, Leslie asked if Lauren Dowdy had any siblings. "An older sister, but she drowned," Evie answered—with a precision that unsettled her mother. "And her parents are divorced, so she can't have any more." One day, the macaw taught Lauren and Evie an obscene word for oral intercourse.

At first, Leslie believed Lauren to be a stand-in for her daughter's disloyal friends—that all it required to banish the imaginary girl back into stardust would be a renewal of Evie's former relationships or overtures from other potential playmates. But when a happy-go-lucky eleven-year-old brunette named Melissa moved into the bungalow across the street and invited Evie to go bowling with her family, Leslie's daughter adamantly refused—because she'd promised Lauren that they'd spend the day together expanding her macaw's vocabulary. Even a phone call from Kim Pitchford went unanswered. "Tell her I'm playing with Lauren," commanded Evie with uncharacteristic ferocity. "Lauren is my best friend now. I don't need *two* best friends." The next week was Evie's own birthday, but she warned Leslie in advance not to purchase a Queen Anne dollhouse—even though she'd been begging for that particular gift all year. "I don't want to make Lauren jealous," she explained—after the other girl had supposedly walked home. "If you buy me a dollhouse, you have to buy her one too. Okay?" Had Evie been somebody else's daughter, this appeal would have seemed touching, even humorous.

Hugh urged her to take Evie's behavior in stride—if you normalize it, she'll grow out of it sooner—but following the dollhouse plea, Leslie suspected that this was more than merely a phase, that her daughter's long-term mental health might be seriously endangered. That night, she waited until Hugh had powered down his laptop and was about to turn off the bedside lamp. (Although she hated confrontation—even preferred her own suffering to an argument—she could stomach an argument for her daughter's sake.) "We need to do something about Evie," she announced. "I know you're convinced this will pass. But it's been three months already, and it's not passing."

Her husband released the lamp switch with reluctance, obviously unenthusiastic about discussing their daughter's psyche. What had initially attracted Leslie to Hugh—his zeal for scientific rationality, his stoicism in the face of crisis—proved exasperating in matters of childrearing.

"It's not causing her any distress," he said. "Why get worked up?"

"It's causing *me* distress," answered Leslie. "I want to take her to a doctor."

Hugh shook his head, grinning. "I *am* a doctor," he said—as she had anticipated he would.

"You're an epidemiologist." They'd had this conversation before—every time she'd suggested phoning their pediatrician over a rash or a fever. "I mean a *real* doctor. Maybe even a psychiatrist."

Giving voice to the word "psychiatrist" somehow made her daughter's condition more critical, like the word "terminal" had once made her mother's lung fibrosis.

"In the first place, four years of medical school says I'm very much a *real* doctor, Mrs. Malansky, thank you very much," retorted her husband. "Probably more real than any half-witted headshrinker. And in the second place, I don't think we're there yet. If you're genuinely concerned, we'll sit down with Evie and figure out what she's really thinking . . . For all you know, she could admit that this Lauren girl is entirely imaginary . . ."

That was Hugh: always a plan, always in control.

The next evening, at bedtime, they again accompanied Evie into her room for a heart-to-heart-to-heart. Leslie sat at the foot of the bed, letting the child rest her pajama-clad legs across her lap. Hugh settled backwards onto an undersized desk chair. He'd been inspecting agricultural sites all afternoon, and he still had a badge reading, "VISITOR – SESTITO'S DAIRY," stuck to his shirt breast. Leslie waited for him to broach the perilous matter of Lauren. Instead, Evie asked, "Am I in trouble?"

"No, you're not in trouble, princess," Leslie soothed. "Hugh, tell her we're not upset with her . . . "

"Of course, we're not upset with you," began Hugh, palms resting on his folded knee, leaning forward like a country physician, his glasses perched halfway down the bridge of his sharp nose. "We're just *concerned*. . . . I know you were upset about the parakeet . . . and about that Pitchford girl . . . "

"Oh, Papa. You're so silly. There's nothing to be worried about," interjected Evie. The girl lay surrounded by plush animals and frilled throw pillows. "Now that Lauren and I are best friends forever, I don't care about Kim. Not at all. Anyway, Kim was a bitch."

Leslie winced. Hugh ignored the profanity. "Your mother and I want to make sure that you realize Lauren is imaginary." Even as her husband spoke, Leslie felt like a monster—as though they had denied the existence of Santa Claus or the tooth fairy.

Evie folded her slender arms across her chest. "She is *not* imaginary. She's standing right there," she cried, pointing with her index finger. "That was mean, Papa. Now you've upset her."

"She *is* imaginary," replied Hugh—his tone remaining level and matter-of-fact. "You're a big girl, Evie, and it's important that you recognize the difference between real things and imaginary things."

"Lauren is not a thing. She's a person," Evie shot back. "Please stop talking about her before you hurt her feelings even more. It's past my bedtime."

Hugh stood up and strode to the door, conveying an air of decision. "You're welcome to play make-believe all you wish, honey.

But from this moment forward, your mother and I are going to treat you like an adult." Reluctantly, after embracing her daughter, Leslie followed him out of the room.

"Now what?" she asked.

"We do exactly what I said," he replied. "She can keep playing with that imaginary girlfriend all she wishes. But that doesn't mean *we* have to."

And Leslie did her utmost the whole day Saturday to comply with her husband's instructions. When Evie boasted that Lauren had received the highest score on Mrs. Driscoll's spelling quiz the previous week, she nodded noncommittally. And fearing that Evie would demand two identical bowls of ice cream after lunch, she asked her daughter to serve the dessert herself. That way Evie, not she, was responsible for the ice cream-flavored soup that she later discarded down the drain. But this impasse could endure only so long, and it finally broke at dinner that evening.

Hugh had been summoned to West Asbury shortly after dawn to investigate an outbreak of food poisoning; he returned home exhausted and cranky following an argument with the owner of a sushi bar who'd refused to surrender the names of his suppliers. Leslie hoped to cheer up her husband by baking salmon in garlic butter, one of his favorite meals. She let Evie do the serving, dodging responsibility for the piece of sizzling fish that went untouched at the fourth place setting. At first, Hugh said nothing. But when he finished his own portion, he scooped the salmon off the extra plate and onto his own.

"Put that back," commanded Evie. "That's Lauren's."

"No, it's not," answered Hugh. "Because Lauren doesn't exist."

A look of anguish colored Evie's features. And then—without warning—she threw her fork across the room into the refrigerator door. The implement clattered to the ground, dislodging several magnets in the process.

Hugh grabbed his daughter's wrist. The girl burst into sobs.

"Please, Hugh," cried Leslie. "You're hurting her."

"I am *not* hurting her," he said. "But we're done with imaginary girlfriends. You can do whatever you wish when you're on your own, young lady, but when you're inside this house, we'll have no more talk of Lauren—or any other make-believe."

"Let go of her," pleaded Leslie.

Hugh relinquished his grip. "I swear, if you pretend to invite that girl home with you again, I'll pretend to spank the living daylights out of her until she can't sit down for weeks. Am I making myself clear?"

Evie said nothing. When Leslie tried to embrace her, she ran to her bedroom and buried her head under the covers.

❅   ❅   ❅

Leslie's daughter did not mention Lauren again. For several days, she roamed the house sullenly, speaking only when spoken to, but increasingly, she requested permission to play with Melissa from across the street and other girls in the neighborhood. To Hugh, this served as evidence that his daughter was perfectly healthy. But Leslie, who'd grown accustomed to having two nine-year-old girls in her home at all hours of the day—first two real ones, then one real and one imaginary—now found the gray silence of the late afternoons disheartening. For the first time ever, she second-guessed leaving her job at the library to play full-time mom. She even considered returning to school for graduate work, possibly acquiring a degree in public health so she could better understand the papers that Hugh published in journals like *The Bulletin of Waterborne Illnesses*. Four afternoons straight, she sat at the bay windows in the living room, reading a novel and periodically peering between the blinds in the hope that Evie might bring one of her friends—real or imagined—home to play. Instead, the girls exited the bus and retreated through Melissa's front door.

On the fourth afternoon, as Leslie gazed in disappointment at the spot where, moments earlier, her daughter had disembarked, a weather-beaten Oldsmobile sedan pulled up to the curbside. It was the species of automobile that Hugh always cursed for its poor gas mileage and environmental impact. "You might as well pump lead into the atmosphere," her husband complained. From the vehicle emerged a broad-shouldered man in his forties, unmistakably handsome, despite a noticeable gut. He drew a final drag from his cigarette, crushed it under his boot, and then strolled up the Malanskys' flagstone walk with his hands in his pockets. Leslie answered the doorbell with a sense of foreboding, as a military mother might greet an unfamiliar officer.

"Mrs. Malansky?" asked the visitor.

She smiled—still clutching the doorknob.

"Steve Dowdy," he introduced himself. "I was hoping you might have a moment to talk about your daughter. Is this a good time?"

At first, she feared he might be an emissary from the school district: a psychologist? a social worker? a truant officer? Yet his last name was all too familiar. Her stomach muscles tightened. "Is something wrong with Evie?"

"That's what I've come to find out," he replied. "I'm her friend Lauren's father. Or her *ex*-friend, it now seems. May I come in?"

Leslie couldn't remember inviting Steve Dowdy inside, but somehow she found herself sitting opposite him in the living room. It crossed her mind that she might be the victim of some sick joke, but neither Hugh nor her brother had an appetite for pranks, and nobody else, other than Evie herself, was aware of the imaginary child's banishment. Listening as her guest revealed his concerns regarding Lauren, in a voice both tender and firm, Leslie knew deep down that this man was not part of any prank.

"She's totally heartbroken," Steve Dowdy explained. "She spends most week nights with her mother, so it wasn't until yesterday that I realized how upset she is." Leslie's eyes dropped toward his strong, confident hands. "You probably think that it's crazy of me to come here like this. My ex told me to mind my own business," he added. "That getting rejected is part of a normal childhood. But Lauren means everything to me, Mrs. Malansky—and it tears my heart up to see her suffering. . . . So I guess I hoped you might be willing to put in a good word for her with Evie . . ." He looked up at her hopefully, and his self-assurance had melted into an adorable sheepishness.

Never in her life had another adult touched Leslie so deeply. She couldn't conceive of Hugh pleading Evie's case to some other girl's parents, if the circumstances had been reversed—certainly not with such humility.

"I'm so sorry," said Leslie. "To be candid, this is my husband's doing. He's a scientist. He doesn't like . . ." She was going to say "make believe," but she suddenly realized how absurd that sounded. Steve Dowdy obviously didn't think his daughter was imaginary—and she *couldn't* be imaginary, could she, if her father was a flesh-and-blood human being sitting on Leslie's sofa? She'd figure out the mystery later, she decided. For now, her goal was to appease her guest. "Hugh has certain prejudices," she tried again. "He was worried that our girls had become too dependent on each other, that Evie wasn't making other friends. And once my husband gets an idea into his skull, you'd have to saw his head off to remove it. I'm afraid he won't tolerate your daughter in our house, at present. But I don't see why the girls can't play together at school . . . " Leslie hadn't intended to run down her husband; an unexpected anger surged into her chest. "I'll certainly say something to Evie . . . I promise."

Steve Dowdy beamed. "That would be wonderful," he said. "I was afraid you might think I was ridiculous."

"I think you're lovely," blurted Leslie.

A hush fell over the living room—pierced only by the distant murmur of the heating system. Leslie toyed with her wedding ring, her eyes focused across the carpet, on the front leg of the piano bench. She sensed heat suffusing her cheeks.

"Lauren was right about you," said Steve Dowdy.

She turned to him in curiosity, also apprehension.

"You *are* beautiful," he elaborated. "More beautiful than I thought possible."

And then he kissed her: The father of her daughter's imaginary ex-best friend, a man who couldn't possibly exist, but whose lips felt far more real than anything she'd experienced in many years. He kissed her, and he kissed her, and then they stumbled to her bedroom. The room was snug, dark, illuminated only through one partially drawn curtain. They didn't bother to turn on the lights. Even while she was enveloped in Steve Dowdy's arms, Leslie also felt outside of herself—a foreigner, watching her own body, dazed by her affection for this alien being. And yet she was happy, maybe happier than she'd been since before Evie's birth.

Afterwards, he sang for her what had once been Lauren's favorite lullaby, a heartwarming tale about a lonely kangaroo who befriends a koala bear.

"Would you mind if I smoked?" he asked.

Under ordinary circumstances, she'd rather have let him sprinkle uranium isotopes inside her refrigerator. But these were not ordinary circumstances.

"I guess not," she said.

"Thanks." He plucked his jeans from the carpet and retrieved his lighter. "I have nothing against public health *in prin-*

ciple," he explained. "But in practice, all the longevity in the world doesn't taste as good as a thick, juicy steak."

Steve Dowdy's cigarette soon filled the room with the cozy scent of tobacco, a transgression somehow even more sinful than extramarital sex. *You're incorrigible today*, Leslie said to herself—but with surprise and bemusement, not guilt. She barely managed to air out the house before Hugh returned home from the office.

❊ ❊ ❊

Guilt arrived soon enough. Steve Dowdy appeared at the same hour the next afternoon, but said nothing of his daughter—and while they were making love, in the double bed that smelled faintly of Hugh's aftershave and socks—Leslie found herself thinking: *I'm having an affair. Me!* The stark tangibility of this fact amazed her. She had known other women over the years who'd confided to her that they'd cheated on their husbands—a garrulous aide in the library's reference room, a former Vassar classmate who'd seduced an electrician—but Leslie felt genuinely baffled to be among these women. The improbability of her role knocked her so far off guard that, during the ensuing week, she nearly forgot that her lover's daughter was supposedly imaginary. In fact, she strove not to think about this enigma. When their conversation drifted to matters that might prove his claims fraudulent, or metaphysically impossible, she steered them back toward the profoundly mundane.

It was inevitable, of course, that Steve Dowdy's outside life would come up during their long talks about love and parenting, and Leslie noted that his stories dovetailed perfectly with what she'd previously learned from Evie. Her lover was a Peace Corps veteran, a part-time psychology professor with a modest private practice. (She even discovered his name and credentials, but not his photograph, on the faculty website for Hager County Community College.) His ex-wife had divorced him for a dental hygienist who'd once been Miss Teen Venezuela and who'd subsequently run off with her manicurist. On the first day Leslie and Steve left the house together—for coffee at the local diner, while Evie attended her weekly violin lesson—her lover described how he'd discovered the body of Lauren's older sister, Amanda, at the bottom of his neighbor's pool. "Patti thought she was with me, and I thought she was with Patti . . . and somehow she climbed through this little gap in their fence," he said. "It was a tiny hole. *Tiny!* You wouldn't have believed a rabbit could squeeze through, let alone a four-year-old." Leslie instinctively clasped his hand, even though they were in a public restaurant, not caring who might see her.

Fortunately, Hugh's public health efforts kept him on the job later than usual that month. On the same afternoon that Steve entered Leslie's life, her husband labored overtime probing a tuberculosis cluster at a chemical plant. Two days later, he phoned to warn Leslie that he'd be home well after dark, as he'd been asked by the mayors of several coastal hamlets to learn whether a colony of low-flying bats carried rabies. Hugh's workaholic fervor, which had so often frustrated Leslie in the past, now afforded her extra time to prepare his dinners. On occasion, she even suspected that he might be faking his responsibilities—that Hugh somehow sensed she was having an affair and, wanting to avoid confrontation, he was giving her a wide berth. Of course, Hugh wasn't a man to avoid confrontation. In fact, he thrived on it. So, more likely, he was too absorbed in his own work to notice her distance. In any case, if her husband did suspect anything, he said not a word. The only time he voiced concerns was that first night, when he inquired whether anyone had been smoking inside the house. "Did you go someplace smoky?" he pressed. "The smell must be clinging to your clothes." After that, she exiled Steve's cancer sticks to the back patio.

Although Leslie had promised that she'd put in a good word for his daughter with Evie, two weeks elapsed before she finally mustered the courage. She truly did want to help Lauren—if the girl even existed—but she feared unsettling her own child, who appeared to have embraced the carefree, rather dopey Melissa as her latest ideal playmate. Leslie finally introduced the subject on a chilly Sunday in November, en route to buy her daughter a new pair of mittens. "Do you ever play with Lauren Dowdy anymore?" she asked—apropos of absolutely nothing.

Evie eyed her suspiciously. "No. You told me not to."

"I know we did," conceded Leslie. "I think your father and I were afraid you were going overboard—preferring her to your other friends. But if you wanted to hang out with her once in a while, especially at school, that would be fine . . . "

She dared not refer to the girl as either real or imaginary. Instead, Steve Dowdy's daughter occupied a narrow passage between truth and fiction.

"Lauren has new friends," replied Evie. "And Melissa is my best friend now."

How intense and fluid relationships were at that age!

But she had done her part. She had *tried*.

What Leslie did not do, on the days she ran into Melissa Steinhoff's mother in the organic market or crossed paths with Rebecca Pitchford at the municipal tennis pavilion, was ask if they knew about a girl named Lauren Dowdy. Because she was afraid of their answers. Because whether Steve was the product of a coincidence or a hoax or a paranormal vortex, she did not want to lose him. She treasured the way her lover asked after every detail of Evie's life—even though she never made similar inquiries about Lauren—and that he probably knew more about her child's daily existence than did her own husband. Besides, Leslie asked herself in a moment of levity, how could their romance be wrong if Steve didn't even exist?

And yet it did feel wrong! She'd been brought up in a traditional home, two parents, one brother, zero imaginary lovers. Duplicity did not come naturally to her, although—for the record—she hadn't actually lied to Hugh about anything overtly beyond that initial cigarette. She hadn't needed to. Instead, her falsehoods were falsehoods of omission, lurking deceptions that festered beneath the pelt of her marriage. She sensed herself in limbo, tugged at from all directions, although nobody was actually doing any tugging. She kept waiting for Steve to demand more of her—even to insist that she abandon her marriage. He didn't. He merely brought her daffodils, and biographies of Carl Jung, and perfect afternoons of seemingly inexhaustible passion. Ultimately, it was Leslie who sought to impose a trajectory upon their relationship.

They had taken advantage of the fourth grade's class field trip to the maritime museum in Seacroft and decided to risk a late lunch at a romantic bistro opposite the Hager Hills harbor. Hugh had been grabbing meals at the office all week, so she didn't even have to worry about his supper. It was a crisp November afternoon—nearly Thanksgiving—and on the stroll across the vacant parking lot, Leslie warmed her hand in Steve's coat pocket. Inside, they opted for a table far from the windows, claiming that they feared the draft. Their waitress lit a candle in a glass jar and handed them each a menu, then sashayed into the kitchen. The only other patron was an elderly, bow-tied gentleman seated at the bar, playing solitaire. He glanced their way for a moment, likely assumed they were husband and wife, and returned to his cards.

"So," said Leslie. "That old man probably thinks we're married."

Steve glanced across the restaurant. "One of us *is* married."

His remark struck her as flippant and she resented it.

"You don't have to remind me," Leslie replied. She took a deep breath, studied the thick veins on the backs of his hands. "Look," she said, "I don't want to ruin things, but I hate running around in secret like this . . . "

Steve nodded. "All right. What *do* you want?"

The problem was that she genuinely didn't know. She didn't want to be having an affair, and she didn't want to leave Hugh, and she certainly didn't want to end her relationship with Steve, but those three sentiments were obviously incompatible. That the enigma of her lover's daughter still remained unresolved only increased her uncertainty. But you couldn't exactly tell a man you'd been sleeping with for four weeks that you weren't sure whether his daughter was real or imaginary.

"I guess I just want to know where we're headed," she finally said.

Her lover traced his fingers along the edge of his menu. His face looked weary in the candlelight. "Do we have to be *headed* somewhere? Can't we just *be*?"

His wish sounded so reasonable—yet so infuriating.

"What *do* I want?" she asked aloud, as though no time had elapsed since his earlier question. "I suppose I want to be a larger part of your life. Sometimes, I feel like I don't know you. We've been getting together like this for a whole month, and I haven't even met your daughter."

Steve's expression turned from worn to wary. "I don't understand. Patti told me Lauren practically spent the entire summer at your house."

This was her moment to demand an explanation, but she lacked the nerve. Blood pounded in her temples. "She wasn't around *that* often," Leslie lied, struggling to recover. She forced a plaster smile. "Hugh used to take the girls with him on his investigations and then drop Lauren off at her mother's on the way home."

No sooner had the words left her tongue that she realized how inappropriate it would have been for her husband to expose another man's child to outbreaks of salmonella and swine flu. Luckily, Steve didn't protest. He still appeared to be digesting her earlier admission about not knowing his daughter.

"I would like to meet her," said Leslie. "Very much. . . . Can I?"

Her lover's expression turned hesitant. "I guess," he replied. "When?"

"I don't know really. Soon."

"How about tomorrow?" pushed Leslie.

Steve shook his head. "Soon," he said again. "Patti and I have a custody agreement. It's complicated. Not something that we can figure out overnight."

Something in his tone, his demeanor, told Leslie that more prevented her from meeting his daughter than merely the logistics of a visit. She didn't raise the matter again during their meal. Instead, they discussed her own father's new "lady friend," and the upcoming PBS documentary about Sigmund Freud, and Evie's progress on the violin—all topics that, at this particular moment, interested neither of them. In the parking lot, she returned to the subject she'd been thinking about through the meal.

"I really do want to meet your daughter," she said. "Can we set a date? Maybe something a few weeks from now . . . ?"

Her companion stopped walking and his entire body appeared to tense up. "I told you: Soon. Why isn't that sufficient?"

She'd never seen him grow irritated before. Rather than causing her to back off—as she might have done with her husband, or almost anyone else—Steve's attitude provoked her.

"I want to name a date," she answered. "A commitment."

Leslie was now fully aware of how unreasonable, even petulant, she sounded.

"I can't give you a date," Steve snapped. Then he paused for a moment, as though collecting himself, and apologized. "I didn't mean to jump on you," he said. "I'm sorry. It's just that Patti has a job offer in another state and everything's up in the air at the moment. She wants to relocate, and she wants to take Lauren with her—and our custody arrangement lets her do that . . . "

"You'd move too?"

Steve gazed into the distance, across the concrete plaza to the masts poking up at the marina. Overhead, gulls circled ominously. "I don't know," he said. "I have a job here—a practice . . . and other things . . ." He looked at her pointedly, a reminder that she was what he meant by *other things*, but his face had lost some of its tenderness.

When her lover failed to appear on her front porch the next afternoon at three o'clock, as he always had, Leslie chose not to phone the number that he'd given her for emergencies—chose not to learn what she might discover at the other end of the line. Even as the winter sun dipped behind the roof of the Steinhoffs' bungalow, she already understood that she'd never see Steve Dowdy again.

* * *

That night, Hugh returned home from the office earlier than usual—his mood sullen and grim. At dinner, he hardly touched his halibut. "Haven't I asked you not to buy fish with high mercury content?" he demanded. "Do you want to turn your daughter into the Mad Hatter? One serving is not going to kill her, but it's a slippery slope."

"I checked the danger list," objected Leslie. "Halibut's not on it."

Hugh frowned. "Well, it should be."

She saw that something must have happened at the health department, but she wasn't in any frame of mind to discuss it; all she'd been able to think about for the past four hours was Steve Dowdy. And although she'd seen him only a day earlier, their entire relationship now seemed a cruel trick of her own imagination. Someday, she might ask Evie about the girl, she understood, or even make inquiries of Rebecca Pitchford and Phyllis Steinhoff— but not yet. Besides, she feared she already knew what she'd learn.

To her amazement, Hugh suddenly inquired after the child.

"Evie," he asked, "Do you ever run into that Lauren Dowdy girl?"

He asked the question as though Lauren were real.

Evie offered him a blank expression. "Who?"

"The friend—the *make-believe* friend—you used to play with. The one who had the invisible parrot . . ."

Leslie's daughter stared at her father intently. "Don't be silly, Papa. There's no such thing as an invisible parrot."

"Obviously, there isn't," agreed Hugh. "But just the same, do you ever . . . *imagine* running into Lauren?"

Evie returned to her food. "I don't know what you're talking about, Papa. I've never had any friend named Lauren. Are you sure you don't mean Kim?"

"No," answered Hugh. "I'm not sure."

They ate the remainder of the meal in relative silence—each of them lost in private thoughts. At first, Evie posed her standard repertoire of questions: How old do seals live to be? What's the difference between *turquoise* and *blue-green*? But even she must have sensed, by Leslie's terse answers, that nobody wanted to talk.

And yet, the moment that Evie excused herself from the dinner table, they both immediately returned to the subject of Lauren.

"She doesn't remember—"

"Probably blocked it out."

Hugh laughed unexpectedly.

"What's so funny?" Leslie asked.

"I was just thinking how glad I am that Lauren's mother turned out to be less of a bitch than Kim's."

That sent a bolt of rage cascading through Leslie's soul. "What is that supposed to mean? How the hell do you know Lauren's mother?"

Hugh grimaced. "That was a joke, Leslie. A joke." He abruptly stood up and began clearing their plates. "For Christ's sake, you sound like you're jealous. Which part of *make-believe* don't you understand?"

"Sure," agreed Leslie. "A joke. Ha, ha."

But the more Leslie reflected upon Lauren Dowdy's mother, and whether she'd had a relationship with Hugh, the less of a joke it seemed. It certainly didn't seem like a joke two weeks later, when she took Evie and moved into an efficiency apartment near the waterfront, or the following month, when her attorney served the divorce papers. What it had been—if not a joke—Leslie could never say. And when she finally did buy her daughter a scarlet macaw, the following summer, she was not surprised that Evie insisted upon naming the bird Lauren. Far better than Quarantina or Malaria, Leslie thought. Far more real.

from *Ghazals for the House*

The soul sometimes leaves the body, then returns.
When someone doesn't believe that,
Walk back into my house.
—Rumi

ii.

Our house has two front doors, side by side, and two mailboxes and
two back doors.
But we use only one of each, since my mom and dad told Mrs.
Bromsky to leave.

There is a large stuffed chair with room for my father and all three
of us kids.
He tells us stories about Bozey, Cozy and Dozey in a land where
rivers run with root beer.

Kids peering through the front door have a straight shot through to
the back door.
Why did the wind not also pass through, but sat outside all the dog
days of August?

When Mrs. Bromsky left, we opened the door between our living
room and hers.
Now we had a Music Room, a downstairs bathroom, and a useless
extra kitchen.

"I know a place where the sun is like gold." My mother plays the
piano, my father the violin.
They harmonize, singing about a place I want to go: "Where the
Four-Leaf Clovers Grow."

Mrs. Bromsky's kitchen is renamed the laundry room, though the
    washer is in the basement.
Boxes of cast-offs fill the room. Where the sink was, a bull-nosed
    pipe juts from the wall.

My father has a record-making machine. A black filament curls up
    from the shiny disk
as the needle plows our voices into furrows: "Twinkle, Twinkle,"
    knock-knock jokes, crying.

iii.

From each side of the house a door opens to the basement.
The dark nook at the top of the stairs collects rags, buckets, stacks
      of newspapers, spiders.

Bachelard believed cellar stairs descend farther and more steeply
      than they ascend.
Our basement steps are backless: open wooden planks floating in
      dusk.

Past the furnace, past the workbench, is the fruit cellar with a
      creaky door and no fruit.
We chalk off a space on the cement floor & tell little kids it's a trap
      door.

From each side of the house, a door opens to the basement: from
      the lively living room and from
the useless laundry room. The washing machine groans in a dark
      corner of the basement.

My father shot a squirrel and skinned it on the workbench.
The tail would have made a good Davy Crockett hat, if Mom had
      let us keep it.

In winter, sheets and pillowcases hang on the basement clothes
      lines, luminous.
In summer the lines are empty; the basement larger; the far wall
      rough, dark.

Hand stretched up, I reach in the dark for the pull-string, hold my
      breath until I find it, jerk it,
banish the crouching unknowns. Where was Bachelard, to hand
      me a lighted candle?

iv.

Inside a door frame, the stairway spirals like the start of snail shell,
        then ascends.
Upstairs, the spindle-edged hallway falls away like a cliff face
        above the stairwell.

On Christmas mornings, we gather at the top of the stairs. Even
        the youngest is given
a lighted candle for the procession. We descend to the tree, singing
        "O Come, All Ye Faithful."

In the hallway linen closet, towels scratchy from line-drying;
        pillowcases with Grandma's
crocheted edges; piles of sheets, my father's pistol nestled in their
        folds.

My brothers' room has two closets. One has a window and a
        clothes rod. Also the cedar chest.
Inside, a ship in a bottle and my mother's satin wedding dress,
        smelling pungent and sacred.

The boys' other closet is long and narrow. A naked cherub sits
        on a shelf. Books, photo albums,
magazines with large-breasted women in black garter belts. The
        darkness throbs.

The door to my parents' clothes closet is always open and bulges
        with layers of my father's
trousers, hanging from the cuffs. I have no closet, just a metal
        bracket mounted on the wall.

My mother keeps her box of Kotex in the corner of their closet.
        When I get my period,
I don't want anyone to know. I sneak past their snoring bed in the
        darkness for supplies.

vii.

Every library book with horses keeps me company in bed: *The
        Black Stallion, National Velvet,*
Misty of Chincoteague. My mother gives me horse knickknacks, but
        tilts her head in wonder.

Fifth grade, sixth — and still reading Grimm. Not so difficult, I
        think, to be silent for seven years
to break the spell that changed brothers into swans. I have been
        practicing silence a long time.

Often the smell of alcohol; hump of moving sheets, creaking. I
        force my breath to be sleep-slow.
Finally their snores. But the pulsing doesn't cease; the throbbing
        now in my young thighs.

The walls of the caves of Chauvet, rediscovered in 1994, undulate
        with horses, their necks
arched, their manes blurred with speed. Unseen since Paleolithic
        days, except in my dreams.

Seventh grade, eighth. In Cinderella, each stepsister cuts off a toe
        or heel to squeeze her foot
into the slipper. It is the cry of birds and the trail of blood that give
        them both away.

Crouched on the black tar roof at night, shadows shift as the
        streetlight swings below. My father
calls and calls my name. I do not answer, claiming this corner of
        the night for myself.

Ninth grade. My older brother and his girlfriend find privacy:
        the laundry room. Empty it, paint it.
No shotgun, but a sudden wedding. Dear Poet, the room, hidden
        in plain view, comes to me.

from *Fox*

"... *the most famous of the* yokai *[Japanese supernatural spirits] are the* kitsune, *who are shape-shifting foxes .... In most stories the kitsune are dangerous, and relations with them lead to madness or death—and yet some kitsune, the* zenko *(good foxes), are said to be wise, intelligent creatures, often poetic and scholarly by nature, who make faithful spouses and are good parents ..."*
—Terri Windling in her introduction to *The Beastly Bride: Tales of Animal People*, co-edited with Ellen Datlow

A White Sun, a Very Cold Sun

so Fox has to squint her eyes almost shut
when she dares the outside, her stomach rumbling
for any food she can find this hard day
of ice, weak snow, air zero.

She treads carefully, her black paws stained
with tiny crystals that can cut off life,
clear eyes searching just the right ways
for rabbit, field mouse, squirrel.

How to survive when the world says no
to breath and whiskers and sturdy tail
dragging weakly through wind like a blaze
of fire so sharp it kills?

Fox is resilient; her temper knows
what it is to be blasted by dark hard fists:
she's rallying now and knows what to say
to smug Death that would take her like this.

Linden Tree

Every three months when the moon's half full
Fox meets him here, the praying soldier,
where clean grass grows tall and lush
and starlings have circled until each has found

its perfect place on a branch. He never has
to open his eyes; she simply makes her red
way to him and lays her muzzle upon
his knees where they bend to touch

strong earth. No matter the season, sky
open or full, he is there and she is there
until dawn calls small dark wings flying.
Fox knows what it is to be a Crone

a lost young man can value: magic
in all that she does not say,
the weight of her head, her amber gaze
what quietly helps him find his way.

from *First Words*

i.

> *Even in Kyoto —*
> *hearing the cuckoo's cry —*
> *I long for Kyoto.*
> —Basho

Even at dawn when dreams and daylight marry
in a Murakami world, our words are spirits who walk
Kyoto silently. Yes, and at dusk we also tread lightly, as if
hearing footsteps would make us disappear.
The past lives inside us here on Shinmonzen-dori. A
cuckoo's voice calls from a clock shop. No hawkers
cry out, only the shuffle of shoppers' shoes—and mine.
I am comfort, I sway under my silks,
long to sing chansons, speak French with the French.
For twenty years I have poured tea, danced, imitated pleasure.
Kyoto, my prison.

ii.

> *Mosquito at my ear—*
> *does it think*
> *I'm deaf?*
> —Issa

Mosquito wings whining
at or near E flat remind me of
my self. What do I want to hear? The closed
ear doesn't & the head does. It listens to what
does the stroking, ignores the rest. Ah, the rest:
it is joy & despair, hope & shame. I sometimes
think the self needs an introduction. A way in.
I'm struggling with an old habit: choosing to be
deaf.

iii.

> *New Year's morning—*
> *everything in blossom!*
> *I feel about average.*
> —Issa

New says change, a thrill or last
year's terror. Your departure leaves every
morning empty. *Is anybody?* you'd say.
Everything we counted on gone, and just
in the middle of quotidian life,
             the dirty dishes, a single
blossom that means to bloom forever.
I water a bud, watch it unfurl,
feel the thorns below, what petals are
about to be. Furled, unfurled like me.
     The day ignores. Sunny, wide open,
average for here. Inside thunderheads.

iv.

> *A sudden shower falls —*
> *and naked I am riding*
> *on a naked horse!*
> —Issa

A day here is a lifetime.
Sudden shadows shift,
shower light on dark until it
falls on sage, spiked cactus.
And the sun falls too, in love
                with the chamisa,
naked, bending in the high wind.
I, like the gray-green leaves,
am longing for warmth,
riding any light shaft I find.
On summer days I lie on
a ledge exposed as the flora,
naked & alert, curry-combed & sleek as a
horse. Nostrils flared, ears forward.

Blueberries on Sugar Loaf

In a false spring, at the backend
of Sugar Loaf where a north wind
has one hard frost left to threaten,
the early harvest sputters tartly.

But I pick along the bushes, pucker
when each blue globe bursts
its skin, and the collected skins
darken my lips and tongue

like some grafted thing,
nearly, newly me, and I believe
it's likely I stain God's tongue,
that all I am is crushed

into a sour, inky pulp.
This is called the good wait.
Then a promised cold snap.
A sudden hand that plucks.

Isla

Una isla que sale de su río con árboles y orquídeas en la cabeza;
guacamayas que hablan idiomas en sus hombros,

una isla aburrida de los barcos, de las gentes que vienen y le dicen
     "hasta luego,"
no quiere nada con los mares que le mandan siempre fotos y
     recuerdos.

Viaja para conocer a los reyes, ir por otros mundos, visitar a las
     estrellas. . .

En su viaje las montañas la saludan, muchos ríos le sonríen, pero la
     isla sigue su camino.

A las ventanas les encantaría abrirle sus brazos,
y seguro que si la isla quisiera, podría entrar a saludarnos.

Pero la isla no quiere, y viaja mientras las ciudades duermen, aun
     cuando la tierra se duerme,

(incluso si el universo bosteza y apaga sus últimas estrellas, la isla
     no se detiene).

Island

An island leaves her river and sets forth with trees and orchids on
      her head;
on her shoulders, macaws change their languages.

This island bored with boats, with people who drop by and say
      "See you later,"

wants nothing to do with the oceans who keep sending her
      memories and photographs.
She's out to meet kings, wander through other worlds, meet the
      stars. . .

On her trip mountains greet her, other rivers smile at her, but the
      island continues her journey.

The windows would love to open their arms to the island;
of course, if she wished, she could stop long enough to say hello.

But the island doesn't want to, and travels while the cities sleep,
      even when the earth itself
is asleep

(even if the universe yawns and puts out its last stars, the island
      won't slow down).

Translated from the Spanish by James Kimbrell and Rebecca Morgan

El amor de las montañas es algo serio

Las montañas aman a cualquier edad. Una montaña con millones de
     años se enamora
de una persona de veinte.

Una montaña dormida miles de años aguarda desesperada un beso
     de cualquiera.

La montaña con el cuerpo en forma de copa quiere que la besen sólo
     los ángeles.

Montañas que aman a otras lo expresan sencillamente a través de sus
     pájaros.

Al mirar atrás, un hombre se da cuenta de que una montaña lo ha
     estado siguiendo.

La montaña que aúlla de amor por las noches es verdaderamente una
     fiera.

Sólo con un poco de arroz y agua cada día, una montaña es más alta
     y más sabia.

(Las montañas de dinero y de ropa para lavar no tienen los mismos
     sentimientos.)

The Love of a Mountain Is Something Serious

Mountains can love at any age. A several-million-year-old mountain
      falls in love with a person of
twenty.

The thousand-year-old sleeping mountain is desperately awaiting a
      kiss from anyone.

A mountain with a body shaped like a wine glass wants only to be
      kissed by angels.

Mountains in love with other mountains express their love simply
      through birds.

A man looks back suddenly and realizes a mountain has been
      following him.

The mountain that howls at night with love is truly *una fiera*.

With a little rice and water each day the mountain becomes the tallest
      and most wise.

(Mountains of money and dirty clothes don't have the same feelings.)

Translated from the Spanish by James Kimbrell and Rebecca Morgan

Brujas

Los pasajeros que viajan de turismo desde Liverpool para Iquitos
        se incomodan
por la presencia de dos brujas en el barco.

"¿Qué hacen estas brujas en el barco? No hay brujas por aquí en
        el Amazonas",
se extraña el capitán, y consulta con la *Enciclopedia Británica*.

"Ellas salieron de unos libros de castillos que leíamos nosotros,"
        confiesan dos niños asustados.

La pareja de Amberes reprende a sus hijos y le pide disculpas al
        capitán.
Las brujas también reciben su regaño y el capitán les ordena
        regresar inmediatamente a su
castillo medieval.

Pero los niños tiraron los libros al río.

"El calor y la humedad del Amazonas nos obligaron a salir volando
        del castillo,"
explican con voz temblorosa las brujas.

Los pasajeros le ruegan al capitán que las lleve de vuelta para Europa.

El capitán consulta con la agencia de turismo de Liverpool y decide
        llevarlas de regreso,
con la condición de que las brujas le ayuden a barrer la cubierta del
        barco.

Witches

Passengers on a ship from Liverpool to Iquitos are disturbed
by the presence of two witches on the ship.

"What are these witches doing aboard? There are no witches in this part
of the Amazon," says the puzzled captain, as he consults the *Encyclopedia
Britannica.*

"They came from some books about castles we were reading," confess two
      frightened children.

The couple from Antwerp reprimands their children and asks the captain's
      forgiveness.
The witches get a good scolding and the captain orders them to return
      with haste
to their medieval castle.

But the children have thrown the books into the river.

"The heat and humidity of the Amazon led us to fly out of the castle in the
      first place,"
the witches explain to the captain in quavering voices.

The passengers beg the captain to take the witches back to Europe on the
      return voyage.

The captain consults the travel agency in Liverpool and decides to take
      them back to Europe
provided they help sweep the deck.

Translated from the Spanish by James Kimbrell and Rebecca Morgan

What Returns

I am religious in my failures
at love: the singular repentance,
the carnal baptism, and then that
falling away again, that slow return
to loneliness—the arrival I'm starting
to think I crave. But the rest

begs back. I loved a girl who pushed
like that, like the sea, her need to know
the lie of becoming a shared body—both
the source and exodus promised.
What I remember most: the way her wrist
filled my hand in the morning, and the salty-

sweet scent of desire—: her hair across her back,
as she slowly dressed from the bottom up.

The Epistemology of Preposition

— after A. Van Jordan

Of 1. "during": As in the 28ᵗʰ day of July, of 2011, L finishes
lifting the 30th and final hour of our son's getting here—and now
I can talk in few tones other than the sweetest day of my life. 2.
"being or coming from": As in L has come to me by way of Florida,
of Cuban heritage, of parents who left one country's darkness
for another's. She smiles in the gray rain of my Seattle, holds my
hand. 3. "belonging to": More than the sound of skin, more than
the clave of tongues, more than the music, L misses the smell of
churrasco, arroz con pollo, moros y maduros, pasteles y cortaditos spinning
in the blue Miami air. When our son nurses, I imagine him tasting
the fleshy pulp of head-sized mangoes, banana hearts bursting in
the backyards of barrios, oranges rolled in coffee-brown hands. 4.
"concerning; about": I know of grief. My father taught me of want,
of waiting—that you can die of waiting. 5. "having or containing":
Of course, I'll take a piece of L's bread, a glass of her wine, of her
water, the tender country of her abdomen—a place where I can lay
my head of worry.

Upriver, Downstream

— for J

I read the water, and the edges
of the water, august poplars

casting shadows along the bank. Insect
hatches sometimes bloom

straight from the riffles —all of it
a wayward map to the trout

flexing just beneath the long arch
of my fly-line querying the current.

Alone, I rifle streamers through pockets
deep enough to hold fish large

as memory. With others, I will wade
waist-deep all day, for the small

paradise of watching someone
run their fingers along the belly

of what was once impossible
to touch. And release everything back.

The Light that Lasts All Summer

Taking out the trash
I stop, bag in hand,
          to look up at the moon —

looking up, of course,
being something real
New Yorkers supposedly
never do, being both too cool
and always in too big
a hurry, thanks very much —
though if true this would mean
we'd miss practically
everything. But here

in the northwest corner
of the Bronx, about as far
as you can go
without saying so long
to the city, all leafy
green on a high terraced hill
in the sharp elbow
of two rivers — mighty
coffee-dark Hudson
and skinny smooth
Harlem — where the mumble-
grumble of the commuter
train's just noticeable

back beyond those trees,
looking up is what we do.
Also looking out, looking in

and over and sometimes
just to survive
taking an unblinking look
at all the things no one
really wants to see:
the man collecting cans
for the five-cent refund
each morning, cart piled high
with bags and boxes,
the sickly sweet smell
of flat Pepsi and stale beer
he can never wash away,
or the grubby-fingered woman
on the 1 train asking each
of us, "Can I get a hand
up, not a handout?"
When she turns to me I see
she's pregnant. My moon-viewing
party's a quick one—the trash
bag's heavy, ripe, the night

crisp and shivery. I've seen
skunks and possums creep out
of these woods. And once
a raccoon, slow and low-
slung, came trundling up
the hundred and fifteen stairs
it takes to climb our hill
as the sun was reeling
up into the sky and I was
trudging down and off
to the subway, to
Manhattan, to work.
He might've been a banker
reeking of booze in his fat
fur coat, sneaking home

after a long night out
on the expense account.
I held my breath: he passed

right by. I'm writing this here
at the kitchen table—
June morning, still cool
and dark, an early start
before the sun leaves us
parched on the pavement—
and remembering trash bags,
raccoons, the steps I retrace
each day, down and up
and down again, because
I want to show you

what life is like in all
its sweet dizzying minutiae,
the simple everydayness
and occasional tang
of wildlife here in what's
technically still the city.
I want to show you these days,
the thousand little things
they're filled with: cloudy rivers
shimmering with sun, old oaks
and elms, Amtrak trains,
the bright surprise of Chinese
music, the erhu's plaintive cry
that makes me lonely for

something I can't name,
hundreds of sparrows gossiping
in an overgrown hedge,
unleashed dogs, coffee light
and sweet, a shouty bluejay
letting his wake-up call rip
through the morning, darkness
and starlight, the way
even during the day
you can still sometimes see
the moon—a mystery
to me, one I would've read up on
just so I could explain it

to you, when you wondered
why too. I want to show you
what life is like here
where you ought to be
with us, but aren't. A not
uncommon story, though few
people will tell you

it's their story too. They choose
not to relive it, relieved
not to revisit what happened
or didn't. What should have.
What went wrong for no
other reason, finally,
than that it didn't go right.
Ours is the story of how
is became *was* and *was* became
wasn't, became *no*,
became *not*. The story
of our almost girl, our mighty
might have been. How our *why
not* became our *would have,*
how *could have* became *can't.*
The doctor closed his chart
and said, "I'm not seeing what
I should see." The smallest heart
I've ever dreamed of
wasn't moving. He couldn't
hear you. I wanted
to hate him, have this be
his fault. The room was too small
and dark and hot and
then I couldn't hear anything
either. Summer's no season

for grieving, it doesn't
satisfy, it's too sunny and warm
and everything just keeps
growing, *burgeoning forth*
as the poets used to say

into stalky shoots of green,
frilly leaves, pink and yellow
flowers, everything's going on
and on and on. Even the crickets
chirp away each night
as if it'll last forever
and they will too, so why not
make music, joyful
noise, let us know you're here
and loving it. You would

have loved the insect market
in Shanghai—that muddle
and crush of booths and
boxes and bins, the pull
and push of an open-air market
but covered over
with scraps of tarp and tin
so that buyers and sellers
alike hunker down,
elbow into the dingy half-light
and bug-hum of commerce.
Hawkers show off
black crickets in plastic vials
and boxes, feeding each
an eye-dropper's worth of sugar
water, the bigger bugs (what *are*
those?) squeezed into
bamboo cages, insects big as

my thumb with whipsaw
legs, serrated, iridescent black
and green, a flash of red
down the back. The dealers up
and coming, or down
on their luck, are booth-less
and table-less: they squat
on the concrete, tiny pots
arranged before them,
lifting each lid to check on

the shiny dark cricket inside—
Still there? Still ready
to fight for your life?
You would have been

an only child like me
or like so many kids in China
these days, those privileged
loners, and so many here
adopted from there,
preparing now for bat
mitzvahs or dyeing
Easter eggs pink and orange,
carpooled to weekend
calligraphy and lion-dance
classes by blond dads,
moms who teach poli sci
at Columbia, wondering—
loved but still curious, loved

but confused by the odd
escapes that shape
our lives—*How on Earth*
did I ever wind up here?
You would have been
an only child like me,
alone and not lonely
most of the time, lost
a little, but mostly
okay with it all—
the living inside the mind,
I mean, the wandering
through the woods,
those half-remembered, half-
imagined woods—

and laughed at this old man,
at *your* old man.
"My *dad*," you'd say. "How
weird," you'd say, "the way

he talks, his love
of books—words on paper,
can you *believe* it?" and laughed
with your friends, of whom
you'd have many
from all over our shrinking
world—smaller still
by the time you arrived
and grew up and started talking

like this. "He calls the end
of the bread the *heel*, remembers
things called *records* and *cassettes*.
Sometimes when he can't
find his glasses, he asks
where are my *specs*?"
You would laugh at this
old man from an older world
already mostly gone,

already over with, the way
the music I love was played
by people dead now
for years, decades, like King
Oliver who shouted
and rasped and rushed golden
notes through his cornet,
his many mutes—derbies and
plungers and bottles and cups—
making a wah-wah wheezing
singing crying human voice
out of his hot breath, so sad
and so sweet for so long
till his teeth rotted and it hurt
too much to play. He ended

up a janitor in a Georgia pool hall
and died too young, busted
and broke, buried—*how on Earth?*
—here in the Bronx, in Woodlawn

Cemetery, not far from Shakespeare
Avenue, where I would take you
just to see the green street sign.
Or Thelonious Monk, who
got so rundown tired and sick
across the river in Englewood
he told his sister, "I just don't feel
like playing anymore"—
not even "'Round Midnight,"
not even "Crepuscule
with Nellie," the song he made
for his wife and always
played note for note, just the way
he wrote it. So he didn't
play, not ever again, his mind
and his piano slowly filling up
with dust. Out in

Ewen Park now, the trees
just one shade darker
than the sky, the fireflies play
hard to get. They blink on
and off, on and
off. They telegraph us
their secrets—

     over here
               over here
over here

       —with their green
glow-in-the-dark bellies. When we
first moved here, Lily and I
stopped in surprise to watch those
here and gone and here again

tiny lights I remembered
from childhood and had never
seen before in the city,
though soon we realized

they come out here all summer.
Someone told me
it's their mating dance
though I never looked it up
to see if that was true

and now we walk right by
in our hurry to get home.
But since this is all just
imagining anyway—reckless
careening around curve
after curve; no brakes, eyes
closed—and since I can hear it
now: your voice, your sweet
laugh that hasn't hurt anyone,
I want to stop here, mid-
sentence, and open my eyes
so I can look at you:

my slight girl, tall and awkward
in glasses, uncertain-seeming
(like your mother) and too quiet
sometimes (like me), so that
people who don't know you,
not really, try to finish
your sentences, rush you
along even though you're nearly
thirteen, as if they've got you
figured out. But steely
underneath—that little crease
between your eyebrows
the giveaway you're sure
of what's what without needing
to say so. Your long brown hair
lightens to honey in summer,
the mysterious chemistry of pool
water and sunlight, something
I would've never figured out

the *how* of and been happy
just to see and love and not try
to explain. Curious about anything
with legs or wings—lizards,
moths and caterpillars, toads, birds,
the broken eggs beneath the oak
that *do* require some explanation.
You're only six, I see

now, sharp-eyed and skeptical
before you have any reason
to be: no one's died yet
you know. You squint when
you smile, you may
need braces, you have a cloud
of freckles across each
cheek, you keep
losing one red mitten
and finding it again, you say
snowflakes taste
like little rivers when
they fall on your tongue

and then a door slams shut
on that other life. What woke

me up? Somewhere
a bell rings. Another door

slams—a literal door now,
wooden and loud. Someone

grinds coffee—*whir, whir*—
lets the water run until it's cold

enough. Lights go on up
and down the hill, first one

and then another and then
another. God *bless* it—

as my father used to
say, angry but not wanting

to swear because
there was a child there—

another day gets going.
What else can we do finally

but get going too?
So I'm here. Still trying to

make what happens make
some kind of sense.

God bless it, I think, this
painful imagining

and then the cold world
we wake to once more.

What comes after—
we keep wondering when

will it start? So here's the rest
of the story I want you to hear:
of course we didn't buy
any crickets. But as we haggled
over the price of a cricket case,
small as a deck of cards
with a sliding lid of curlicued
wood over a plastic window
so you could see

your cricket sitting there
(legs angled in, antennae
aquiver), the cricket-seller—
a young woman who knows
how old, eighteen, twenty-
eight? She was someone's

daughter, her cap pulled
low, ponytail sprouting out
the back — offered
to throw in a free cricket
to seal the deal. Perfect

souvenir of a faraway world,
I thought I'd keep my case
pocketed like a worry stone
I could rub to wear away
my worries. I'd keep it empty
but at the ready. As I held it
and turned it over,
looked at it and tried to decide —
too expensive, I thought, too
wonderfully useless
for me, though if I said no
when would I ever
have the chance again?

—an old man squeezing
through the crowd paused
and turned back. Two bent
and wiry hairs stuck out
of his cheek. A long life,
this means in China, if
you don't pluck them. He said
something to the woman
and pulled from his pocket —
like a perfect moment's

magic trick — his own
identical case. He slid back
the cover to show me
his mechanical-looking cricket
waiting there. His smile
said he appreciated
the coincidence, this chance
to show it off — I couldn't tell you
how, but I could tell

his cricket was a prized one,
a scrappy survivor.
He was happy in the *right now*
of this moment. He loved
his cricket even if
or maybe just because
they only ever live a few weeks
and so, unable to sleep,

I step back out
empty-handed now
to look once more at the moon.

Shoshana Kertesz, "Hudson River," photograph

Safe House

My mother tells the story, over and over, so it will never be forgotten. I was still safe inside her when the bomb hit our home. The explosion pushed her down and she said I tumbled inside her, like a bird falling from a nest. She crawled through the broken pieces of glass to find her father and mother who were crouched down together when the roof fell down. It was so dark, she said. She cut her hands, her face. Above her, she saw the green streaks in the sky just before another flash. The sheep in the hills were terrified, calling to one another. My mother told me she heard her own parents crying like frightened children as she tried to save them.

Entezaar. Entezaar. Who was she telling to wait? When she finally found them she put her mother's hand on her belly. Wait. Wait. I could not wait anymore. I came out and my grandmother's cold hand touched me; I can feel it, even now. But I was too late. If only I'd come sooner would they still be alive? My mother had wanted a boy, but she said I was a brave girl that night. I did not cry. I was probably too scared to cry. All my mother could hear was the sound of explosions farther away and the planes flying toward Kandahar.

The twin towers had come down.

"Operation Enduring Freedom" had begun.

❖ ❖ ❖

My father was working for the Americans in Kandahar, translating Pashto and Dari for them. They had told him his village would be safe. But they made a mistake. A terrible American mistake. And so, they promised to relocate him, and us. To a safe house in a place called Virginia. It was very far away; it took another year to get there.

But something happened between Kandahar and Virginia. My mother had a dream and I had the same one. My last dream in Afghanistan. Or maybe she told it to me so many times it feels like it came from me. Our family followed the teachings of Zarathustra: *Good thoughts. Good words. Good deeds.* Truth must win over lies. My grandfather had wanted to be buried in the sky, on top of a Tower of Silence. The dead were placed there, on the flat roof. Three circles, one inside the other: one for men, one for women, and the smallest circle for children. This is the ancient way, to give the gift of the dead to the birds so the earth will not be contaminated. So the spirit can fly free.

There was no tower left for them. My mother had had to bury her parents in the ground the year before and now that we were going to America she said she could hear them calling to her, crying that they did not want to be left in the dirt where so much blood had been spilled. When I think about my grandparents, I hear them crying, too. There is still nothing I can do to help them. They only wish for light, for air. "*Khod☐ H☐fiz,*" my mother said, to her parents, to her country. She said she had failed them. *If only* became my prayer.

✳ ✳ ✳

We came to Alexandria, in Virginia. My mother said it was a good omen, that our new city had my name. Our safe house looked safe. It was made of brick, two stories high. It had a flat roof you could get to by the stairs. My father told me he carried me up there the first night. He could see several stars through the clouds. There were no mountains for the moon to hide behind. He could not hear sheep anywhere. In the living room below, my mother turned on the TV and it was loud enough to drown out the cries of her parents who had followed her there.

My father set me down on the roof and smoked his first American cigarette. Just then, there were firecrackers from another roof. He told me that I began to cry. He gave me the keys to the house to play with, to distract me. He said he knew then that I would become an artist because I made white scratches in the black tarpaper, scratches that reminded him of birds in flight.

But when I hear him tell this story I only feel sad. I see myself as a baby, scratching away on a rooftop, a place safe enough, finally, to cry.

❊ ❊ ❊

I am almost eleven years old now, as old as the war. My father drives to work like any other American father, only he goes into Washington, D.C. He leaves early, comes home late. I hardly get to see him. My mother does not drive at all. I help her shop on the Home Shopping Channel with credit cards. I translate her orders because she still speaks only Dari. The table next to her TV chair is full of lotions and special creams. None of them help the scars from the glass that cut her face in Afghanistan.

No matter what we do, how hard we try, my family will never be real Americans. My father wears a flag pin. My mother has a picture of Barack Obama taped in the window. But people don't trust us. One of the neighbors moved away, I think, because of us. They're not sure what country we come from.

Someone put dog shit in our mailbox once. Someone even threw a rock at the window. It didn't break. There are people in America who want to hurt us. Who want us to go home. They don't know we *have* to be here.

In our house we have a special, secret room, the Afghanistan room. We leave our shoes by the door. My mother and I keep candles lit and make sure the flames don't go out. I help her put up pictures of the mountains near the village of Nadahan where both she and my father were born. Where I was born. Also, we have pictures of my grandparents on the wall underneath a picture of a *faravahar*, a guardian spirit with enormous wings. He holds the circle of truth in his hands. We ask him to protect all of us. I have learned most of what I know about Afghanistan in this room.

Still, I'd like to also be American but my father won't let me have a smart phone. My mother lets me watch TV only some of the time and never the programs with either of the wars. They don't want me to be *too* American. But I stopped calling them *maadar* and *paadar* as soon as I learned English. It's hard to be from two countries.

My father says I should be grateful to go to school, that in Afghanistan, girls can't, because of the Taliban. Sometimes I wish I was still there. This year, I didn't like my teacher and so I didn't study as much as I should have. My grades were terrible. My father wants me to do better, to take extra school so I can bring special honor to the family. He doesn't say it but I know. In America, I have to be more than my mother. So I have to go to summer school. Most of the kids there are mean. Many of them have problems. I never get picked for teams and they call me "raghead." As if I wore a turban instead of a scarf! It's hard to have good thoughts. Good words. Good deeds. Sometimes I just want to hit someone.

❖ ❖ ❖

I stay up late until my father comes back from work so I can tell him what I learned in school today, how people came to watch the start of the Civil War. They sat on a hill with picnics as if a red curtain would open on the movie of the Battle of Bull Run.

He says that war is an American sport. With teams. In Virginia, if you're not from the South, they call you a Yankee. He says people don't know what to call him at the State Department.

But I know. I try to tell my father the names I've been called. Especially the one I was called in the cafeteria today. I was sitting with the kids from other countries: Syria, Lebanon, Iraq. They're not problem kids, just not very good in English. An older boy came over to us and said, pointing at us, "Sand niggers. I'll bet you're all suicide bombers. You're probably going to blow up the school."

I sat there and turned to stone, my fists like rocks. I wanted to shout, to fight. Like a boy. All I did was watch and wait like a girl. But I could feel a fire get started inside me and I didn't want it to go out.

I should have at least tried to punch him but there was a group of boys behind him, waiting. They think we're all *jihadis*. One boy with a military haircut shouted *"Semper Fi!"* but I didn't understand. It sounded like Latin. I won't be taking Latin until the seventh grade. He stood right in front of me and said in plain English, "If my brother dies over there it'll be because of you."

I have to know. I ask my father now, "Is it true? What did he mean?"

"Alexandria," my father says to me. He puts his hands on my shoulders and looks into my eyes. Finally, after a long time, he says, "It is not true. It is only what he believes. You are not to blame for the death of anyone."

I want to believe him. But I don't know what the truth is anymore or who gets to tell it. The only thing I'm sure of is I don't want to cry like a girl in front of him.

I take off my shoes at the door to the Afghanistan room. It's quiet enough to think in here and the candles never go out. *If only. If only.* I hear a tapping on the wall. It has to be my mother. She taps again. I tap back. She taps once more. I can't explain it. It makes me feel better. To know she is there, on the other side of the wall, sending me a signal from across the world. I know you. I know. Never forget your name.

❊ ❊ ❊

Because my mother had been so sure I would be a boy she named me for Alexander the Great. He named Kandahar after himself as he traveled the Silk Road. My mother often told me the story of his birth, how, when he was still inside of *his* mother, a bolt of lightning struck her belly and a great light came from inside her. She knew her son was no ordinary boy. That his greatness would conquer the world.

The explosion that came just before I was born pushed me out into this world. My mother said she knew I wouldn't be ordinary, either. I was so quiet when I came into the world but I was talking in sentences by the time I was two. I could read music by the time I was four. I could draw pretty pictures by the third grade. But how can a girl defend the honor of her family?

My mother still calls me *Kandahar*. In this way, she calls to me and also to her country. I try to remember from when I was a baby, but other than what my mother teaches me, I have to learn what's going on now in Afghanistan on the Internet at the library, on the wall of TVs at Best Buy, on the news my father watches for ten minutes before my mother takes the remote and changes the channel.

Tonight, she does not change the channel because there is a picture of the village of Nadahan on CNN. People are crying and shaking their fists at the sky. The man on the news is saying that a bomb exploded at a wedding party. The camera shows rows of people wrapped in white sheets on the ground, red blood leaking through.

I look at my mother. She's too afraid to make a sound. For the first time in my life, I see my father cry. We are *from* there. He met my mother there. It's the same town where I was born. And now all those bodies are touching the ground.

The man on the news is saying that no one knows what happened. It could have been the Taliban. It could have been Pashtun tribal leaders taking revenge.

It could have been an American bomb, another mistake. That had happened before, planes bombing another wedding because the men were shooting in the air to celebrate. But there had been no shooting yet in Nadahan. They had just sat down to share their dinner.

The man telling the news says, "Wait, we have just had a report. It was a suicide bomber. A thirteen-year-old Muslim boy." The man sounds almost relieved—America is not to blame. A witness tells what happened, with a woman translator's voice a few seconds later like a strange echo, as if she's speaking from inside him. The boy was dressed in white, for the wedding. He walked into the house, into the room where the men were sitting down to the feast. They greeted him. They made a place for him at the table. But the boy just stood there, staring at them. He started to reach under his shirt. He looked frightened.

They knew.

His hand kept searching for something as they all jumped up, knocking chairs over to run. The men were shouting, trying to get out of the door all at once. And then. And then.

I already know how it ends.

I have to get out of the living room. I need to go outside but at night it's not safe, my father always says, so I can only go up to the roof. I run up the stairs as fast as I can.

A few stars shine through clouds. I can't stop thinking about Nadahan. Nothing should grow from that ground the next spring. That's what my grandfather would say. There is nothing left of that boy to put inside the smallest circle on the Tower of Silence for the birds to forgive. But now he will live forever as a martyr, maybe. The wings of the *faravahar* could still fold around him.

I look for the chalk I used to keep in a coffee tin to draw pictures in the black tarpaper. Pictures drawn by a baby. Sheep. Trees with fruit. Mountains with snow on top. Birds that fly in the night. All the letters of my long name. But rain has washed those pictures clean.

If only. If only.

I am not a child. Just a girl. With the white chalk I scrape a circle large enough to hold her.

When I go back down to the living room my father and mother are sitting close together on the couch. My father's eyes are closed. My mother takes the remote from his hand. She changes the channel. But she pushes the "scan" button by mistake and so the TV flips from one channel to the next, looking, looking for something. A basketball game. A police show. Someone cooking. An opera. A black and white movie of a woman on a train. A commercial of a cat with a crown on its head eating its food. A man standing at a distance from a car and pointing a remote at it—the car blows up, a ball of fire shoots into the sky; the man smiles. Another commercial of a boy in a kitchen with a remote in his hand. He points it out the window at the car in the driveway. The car starts. The boy smiles.

I take the remote and turn the TV off.

My mother's eyes are closing, closing, closed. My parents breathe deeply, together on the couch. *"Maadar. Paadar."* I whisper. They're the most beautiful words in the world.

Remember your name, my mother would say. What would *Kandahar* do?

I go into the Afghanistan room to make sure the candles are still lit. I look at the picture of the *faravahar* with his wings spread wide and ask him for protection. He seems to be saying, *"Entezaar. Entezaar."* But I can't wait any longer.

I'll find the walkie-talkie that my father got for me when we went hiking once in Rock Creek Park. He must have wanted a boy, too. We took different trails. After about an hour my father's voice came through the walkie-talkie from half a mile away. "Alexandria—can you hear me? It's time to go home. Over and out."

It's just a toy. It will have to do.

❊ ❊ ❊

In the morning before school, I sneak past the kitchen, past the breakfast my mother made for me. I can't eat. She won't see. She's sitting in front of the television like any other day. My father has gone to work.

I find the duct tape I need in my father's toolbox. I go back upstairs and wrap the walkie-talkie to my chest and the tape makes a ripping sound as I unwind more and more of it. I tear the end off with my teeth.

I put on my best white blouse. White pants, too. My blue and red Nike shoes.

On my way out of the house I take the remote for the DVD player. My mother won't need it and besides, she doesn't know how to work it without me. She knows only the one for the TV.

I walk all the way to school and count my steps. 3,012. By the time I get there it's lunchtime and I walk straight to the cafeteria. But lunch must be almost over. I hear the bell ring. Most of the kids are leaving. I see my new friends, Jamal from Syria, Mina from Iraq. They're just getting up from their table. They wave to me. Then I see the boys who don't like us, sitting where they always sit, by the window in the corner. They're not in a hurry to get anywhere. They're still eating.

I walk toward the boys' table and stand about ten feet away. They ignore me. I come a little closer.

The boy who said *Semper Fi* yesterday looks up. "Why are you wearing your pajamas? Did you escape from the mental hospital?" He tears the tip off a new slice of pizza. He's got braces on his teeth.

I just look at him. I'm not afraid now. He has no idea. None of them do.

I reach my hand under my blouse. I turn the switch of the walkie-talkie on. The scratchy sound of static comes from somewhere inside me and it sounds like a long, long fuse burning toward a bomb. The boys stop chewing.

I know I'm out of range, but I wish my father's voice could come through the speaker right now. *Alexandria. It's time to come home. You have hurt no one.*

But there is no voice. And Jamal and Mina can't help me now. They don't speak English.

I think of the boy in Nadahan, watching the men try to get up from the table and run for their lives. These American boys just sit, frozen to their chairs. The way I did yesterday when they called me terrible names. They don't know, not really, because there is no bombing at their weddings, at the Metro, in the parade of the Fourth of July. But they know all about superpower. I have it now. *If only* turns into *I don't care.*

I take the remote out of my back pocket. I point it at *Semper Fi.*

His face goes from a sneer to a question to total fear.

I would be afraid if I were him.

But I would also be afraid if I were that boy in Nadahan. Now I can see him, the sweat on his forehead. I can feel his hand shaking as he searches for the pin. He knows the sound of an explosion—was he born in one, too, like me? He's almost home. How much longer? A whole second? Until he becomes a ball of light and thunder, a shooting star. He breaks apart to fly in all directions like the red seeds of the pomegranates that will grow in the hills of the village of Nadahan by spring.

I press the red button in Virginia.

Nothing happens.

But everything is about to change.

We'll be safe. For now.

Glenn Herbert Davis, photograph

In My Native Home

Fukushima, March 11, 2011

1

Family. Safety. These too are waves.

Then I drive back to our home,
and lock myself into this miraculous
catastrophe.

Because one. Horizon shift.
A small wave mocks itself big.
Debris answers.

Because radiance lives here too.
War without war. Within this
wayward radiation.

A trembling beyond a home's despair.
Despair just a backdoor stoop.
Up or down. Because number three.

Particles, waves, walls—
I lay down each breath within you.

Sartre, I challenge every no exit
noun verb page you wrote.

Shi no tsubute (pebbles of poetry).
"Can there be any meaning in causing
us such pain?"

Shi no kaikou (encounter of poetry).
"What can we believe if it teaches us nothing?"

Shi no mokurei (silent prayer poetry).
"Shh, petals falling to the ground. Night."

2

Stupidly, I raise my twitter fist,
blurt I can tell a better story
than any quake, wave, or radiance.

"The ocean was sitting around one day,
thinking up jokes. The water down under
is a trickster kind of guy."

The tsunami was the punchline.

Because I want to laugh too.
Because I want to gallop too.

Like a bump on a log.
Or maybe two bumps.
One for each eye.

Like two bumps inside a log.
So the log can laugh
as it crashes through our town.

All God particles—the ones
inside the crashing—are being
and nothingness free.

Because the white whale is not white.
Color of killer debris.
Color of "once in a thousand years."

Each petal word, whale word,
even to the most fearful among us,
offers a wave way through.

Twitter out, twitter in,
each poem an angel of history.

"Shh, it's an aftershock. Millions of horses
are galloping underground, crying."

Radiant Evacuees

A clock sweeps up on another clock,
an alien beach. Sand.

A clock sweeps up on bigger, smaller,
another second hand.

❊ ❊ ❊

"Radiation is falling." Radiant milliseconds
splash and sparkle all around us.

They drive us out of our native place,
cruel, as if we were foreigners.

Why are we being punished,
one step, one breath and the next
interrogated? We have done nothing
wrong. But live.

Particles. S-h-h, particles.
Can we walk into the ocean without hate?
These contaminated waves, a second
hand's revenge.

❊ ❊ ❊

1500 Dai-ichi frogs in a pond,
"too fragile to withstand an M-7 earthquake"

❊ ❊ ❊

The radiation clocks "are falling to the ground
one by one . . . Night."

Dai-ichi, so much depends upon

a wave   a particle   millisecond

calling   or not

the next one.

Survivor Ocean, Suicide Sea

a psalm

Pray rise, reach, now overreach.
Cresting, yours. Collapse of it, yours.

Again and again, time spires
a desperate shimmer.

If I cannot enter, what God
shall I pray to, the God of Cesium 137,

the God of Plutonium 239?
Godzilla's story is Godzilla's joke.

I shall not want. I shall not want.
Why has your shimmering spared me?

What promise of yours could I
possibly keep in the next nanosecond

or two? Though I lie down in darkness.
Dark bodies keep their word.

The Cartographers Conspired

Given the state of maps then, it is hardly
surprising that so many ships failed to return. . .
—William Manchester

Scientists around several tables
decided the planet Pluto isn't.

This is how the cosmos is nudged
by naming, why maps are

complicated, then discarded.
Perhaps it's nonsense to think

of Dante now and where
he happened to place his Hells,

or how the seven visible spheres
became crowns for ancient kings.

And if the Vatican is correct, the Virgin,
ascending at the speed of light, hasn't

left our galaxy yet. This is how
the universe swallows both

regular and immaculate conceptions
without saying excuse me. Still,

we look up often and constellate
stars and read them like tea leaves

because magnetic North, among
other fixed things, is moving.

Confession: I love those early maps
of the unfinished, half-assed world,

unknown places populated by
cryptoanthropological creatures

drawn more carefully than continents
and the pirate syntax of *Here*

There Be Monsters. Marco Polo
was correct to see Chinese unicorns

instead of Rhinoceroses and
never mention drinking tea. This is

the lot of wonder, always pushed
to our peripheries. Yesterday

Google reduced our hometowns to fields
and streets and perfect squares.

Unless we close our eyes we can't
find where we used to be anywhere.

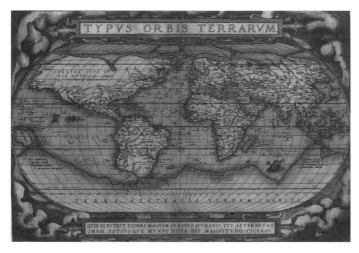

Abraham Ortelius, *Typus Orbis Terrarum,* 16th-century map

California Rain Song

Rain is tinning the roof of the old chicken coop
      where doe and fawn shelter.
         They forage

under the wild plum tree that grew back from root stock
      after a lawn-mower topped
        the apricot graft.

Rain questions neither graft nor stock
       in its glissando down the trunk of the fig,
         first crop of the Fertile Crescent,

coaxes California poppies, free of sleep's swollen satchel,
      twangs lemon leaves, and drops
        a soft percussion on the rind of its fruit.

Though rain has swept through the mountains of Asia,
      it cannot recall the provenance
        of citrus astringent, sweet or bitter;

it does not ask if the spines
      of the prickly pear are redundant
        outside the desert.

There is no discussion in rain's polyphony;
      it nourishes what is here,
        the cultivated and the wild:

calla lily, oxalis, clover, bluegrass, sage bush,
      fescue, fennel, rosemary, black bamboo, blackberries,
        manzanita, juniper, avocado, persimmon, kiwi. . .

What does rain dissolve from the air that seeps into root and leaf?
      What transpires again from leaf to air?
        What gravitates?

In sodden clay, water collects and percolates
        past gopher skeletons, reptilian slough,
            shards of glass, plastic pots,

and the mouth of a buried well—a corona of stones.
        What leaches from the past
            into the current underground?

I must ask, though rain will not tell me
        the story behind the snapshot
            my husband found in our living room:

a teenage boy with glasses, braces and an awkward smile.
        The elderly woman who sold us the house
            returned, and took the photo back in silence.

I can only guess the subterranean path of rain
        by signs of unsettling earth:
            buckled concrete, tilted walls.

Streams seen and unseen run downhill, perpendicular
        to the old cow path from ranch
        to slaughterhouse.

Did the same streams run through these hills when the first cowhands
        slaughtered cattle, kept the hides for leather
        and exposed the flesh to grizzlies?

Cattle gathered by creeks for shade and water,
        trampled the streambed contours,
            left fish in riffles with no shelter.

Where grasses and wildflowers once paved the hillside,
        eucalyptus now grows. An investor scattered
        millions of seeds.

New-growth eucalyptus would *chip when planed
        and crack when dried,*
            its leaves form crowns of fire.

I leaf through time, where words patter;
        drops collect into rivulets from colophon to gutter.
           There are rivers older than the mountains rising in their path.

Where a creek slowed into estuary, above high tide,
        water heaped alluvial on a mound
           overgrown with brambles.

Men carved into its eastern side,
        dissected the cone's curved face,
           with straight railroad lines.

The train whistle had the pitch of keening, timbre hollow
        as the human bones in the mound,
           porous as the bones of the shorebirds above.

Rain quavered through silt, gravel, and two millennia of bones:
        gopher, raccoon, wildcat, deer, elk, wolf, grizzly bear,
           cormorant, turtle, skates, thornback. . .

No. 6 Grave of a child a little over a year old
        found in the tunnel in stratum VIIa
           at a depth of 17 feet below the surface.

It lay from north to south upon a bed of charcoal and red earth. . . .
        A number of shell beads. . . lay in rows from the neck down
           along the body and were originally necklaces. . . *

Men came again, truncated the mound, and raised a pavilion
        to waltz on bones. The creek trilled on as couples danced
           on skeleton pairs buried thigh to thigh,

and mothers whose fetuses had never seen light.
        Rain alone could not wash away these bones.
           The maw of a steam shovel swallowed the mound.

---

* Italicized text is quoted from *The Emeryville Shellmound* by Max Uhle, University of California Publications, 1910, and *Bay Nature*, July-Sept. 2005.

A paint factory rose, stained mud red beyond cleansing,
    redder than ochre sprinklings
        on bones rubbery with lead and arsenic.

What can rain dissolve? Silence is the rustle of shopping bags.
    Spoonbills sleep, beaks buried in wings.
        Metal cranes rest across the inlet.

Where the tide leaves salt crystals on grass, a red-tailed hawk circles.
    A chant evaporates into the air,
        recollecting scattered bones.

From the collection of the Co-Editor-in-Chief, photograph

Warp and Weft

There was no slack in the warp and weft
    my husband's great-grandma
        ran her fingers over.

A *burler* in a Rhode Island mill,
        her job was to feel
            for knots in the weave.

She wore her fingerprints away
    and her skin to such thinness
        blood might seep through.

Did the hours pass evenly
    in the rumble of the loom:
        again, again, gaining

in its appetite for cotton?
    Her father-in-law had returned
        from war and Confederate prison,

to careless workers dropping scissors
    from the upper floors of the mill
        through slots where the driving belts ran.

The weave rended time after time.
    If that happens again I shall quit
        and never work in a mill. . .

It did, and he did,
    wrote his grandson,
        my husband's grandpa.

My father taught me a knot he learned
    as a boy, mending clothes
        when thread was scarce,

and he was left with only
      half an inch of thread
           between cloth and needle.

The needle could not flex,
      so he used the eye to lead the thread
           back through the loop, and tightened it.

Thread took no extensions,
      unlike the *iron thread* he salvaged
           on the streets of Wanchai

and soldered with rosin-scented flux.
      He cobbled together a radio
           where current flowed

through node and wire alike:
      threads of logic
           under music *cantabile*.

When my father first showed me
      a logical loop, I didn't
           follow the syntax.

For i = 0 to i <10
      i = i + 1
Next

I got the drift,
      as in the increment of age,
           the cycle of monsoons;

I like to study iteratives:
      from *crack* to *crackle*, *drip* to *dribble*,
           wrest to *wrestle*.

I condense the cacophonous words
      between my parents
           into a single frequentative.

My father built circuits
    to turn speech into hexadecimals
        my mother couldn't decipher.

For a living, I have learned to code
    in a language where objects
        are discrete,

and strands
    of my mother's hair
        are not allowed to enter.

There are burls in my logic,
    stray insects so small I can't feel
        with my fingertips.

A roving of discarded hair
    and insect wings, I weave
        for my children to ravel.

Quilters

My grandmother's house smells of flea powder
and mothballs, old-lady rouge and last night's beef stew.
She sits in a stiff-back chair—one part of a five-sided
arrangement with her four quilting friends—
chairs pulled close in the middle of the living room,
knees nearly touching one another's—
the old women themselves arranged like a quilted star
sewn from scrap fabric on a twelve-inch square.
Her smelly dog Vincent lies asleep under her chair,
squeezed tightly into a spot too small for his fat-sausage body.
On the floor, piles of leftover fabric remnants—
colorful cotton prints from which the women pick
and choose—fingers never pausing from the serious
work of crafting form from scrap.
The living room, scalloped with sunlight—over-bright
and over-warm—floral-print drapes pushed open to their
limit on every window.
And, when I walk through the living room and into
the kitchen, my grandmother's friends begin to grill her:
Has he moved back in? Did he lose his job?
Did his wife kick him out? Is he drinking again?
These women, all widows, have known me for over
forty years—known my secrets, looked inside my soul.
In small ways, they helped my grandmother raise me
after my dad was killed and my mom threw in the towel.
In their minds, they own a piece of me.
I can hear my grandmother answering *no* to all their
questions, telling them she called me to come
help get her affairs in order—to help arrange the pieces,
as she says. Nonetheless, I hear her making the usual
old excuses: *A good boy, really. A rough life.* So on
and so forth. Her son, my father, stepped on a land mine

in Vietnam when I was four, and it's all
the excuse I've ever needed. For anything.

In the kitchen, the counters are loaded with empty canning
jars waiting to be filled—blue-green glass, fish-eyed and
lifeless; wire baskets loaded with ripe tomatoes waiting
to be stewed and vacuum-packed. A pressure
cooker, on top of the stove, waiting.
And photographs—everywhere—framed, propped up on
the counters, on top of the refrigerator, hanging on the walls.
Photographs of my grandparents, of me as a child.
Photographs of my father as a young boy,
a high school graduate, a soldier in uniform.
A quilt of photographs, a stew.
My only memory of my father is his funeral—
the bugler playing taps, soldiers folding the flag,
handing it to my mother.
I still wonder if anyone arranged
his pieces before they buried him.

I can hear the old women debating whose turn it is to
sew the finished blocks together, to do the
finish-work on the quilt—their voices traveling in
fragments like an echo through the kitchen.
Vincent wanders in—arisen from his stupor—his horned
toenails drumming across the linoleum.
On the refrigerator door, a photo of my mom and dad,
their wedding.
My grandmother is determined that she be allowed to die
in this house, no matter what—that she not be shipped off
to some remote corner in some remote place—and she's
made me promise that I will see to it.
She's told me our souls are pieced together
from this and that, from where we've been and where we're
going—vacuum-packed inside us, waiting to move on.
Souls like stewed tomatoes.
She's told me that the human heart is fragile, but the spirit
remains intact when it departs a broken body.
These are the things she says to me when I visit her,
when we are alone, sitting together in her living room

at night, just the two of us and Vincent, floral-print drapes
pulled tightly closed, dim light filtering around us through
brittle, yellowed lampshades—moth light; empty, stiff-back
chairs pushed to the corners, to the walls.

And she still blames herself for letting her son go to war
when the sons of her friends did not.

Now, I open the refrigerator door. Vincent waddles over.
The shelves inside are full beyond full—remnants of this
and that—too much stuff in a too small space.

Vincent and I stick our heads inside. Together,
we scout the landscape for leftovers.

From the collection of the Co-Editor-in-Chief, photograph

Dirty Laundry

A certain charm about my father. That's what
people said. That's what I'd always heard.
The two of us walking hand-in-hand down the
sidewalk, the top of my green and gold
Kansas City Athletics ball cap reaching barely
above his waist, a white letter "A" above
the bill, women's eyes up and down,
then up and down again. Even I was his currency —
nothing melts women like a handsome man with
a cute kid. Tricks of the trade. Learn it young.
Truth is, women want it. Want it bad.
And he's selling if they're buying. Or vice versa.
A tall man, as graceful and awkward as a giraffe —
knees and elbows churning like piston rods —
like a teenage boy whose body suddenly outgrew
the boy — stirring, somehow, to the female heart.
Always ready to deal, he carried his charms like
a wad of bills in a money clip — his smile, his laugh,
the meticulous suit, his cute kid beside him. Peel off
the charms like tens and twenties, lay them on
the table. Mom had seen through him long ago —
kicked him out, divorced him — so Saturdays were
his and mine together. Men about town.

The day was ours. Rolling through town in his green
1958 Buick Roadmaster, smooth as silk, its chrome
grill locked in a forced grin, the two of us secure in
its thick, cushioned interior, warm in the freedom to go
anywhere, to do whatever we pleased. The doughnut
shop for breakfast. Running errands. Pausing along
the way to talk to everyone he knew. After lunch,
going together to his office at the bank where I sat
powerfully behind the teller's window, counting
and rolling loose coins in paper sleeves while
he made phone calls from his office and did his
paperwork. The bank was closed on Saturdays —
the great foyer was dim — the high ceiling, the tall

windows with the blinds drawn down,
Mrs. Ruby Deschard moving about—shining the
crystal chandeliers, polishing the marble floor,
dusting the walnut-paneled walls and the hulking
cherry-wood desks. Mrs. Ruby—famous about town
because her father had been lynched from
the 2nd Street bridge long ago, when she was
four years old—1929—two days after Black Tuesday—
lynched by an angry crowd because he'd been
disrespectful to a white woman.
While my father worked, Mrs. Ruby made over me,
called me Mr. Little Man, gave me cookies she'd
baked at home that morning, told me that
someday I would run the bank, like my daddy,
like my granddaddy before him.
She told me about her children and grandchildren,
told me about her father—showed me a photo of him
as a young man. Once, secretly—making me
promise not to tell—she showed me a small
black-and-white photo she kept hidden in
her purse—the massive 2nd Street bridge—its intricate
latticework of girders and beams—its back arched
like a cat ready to fight—the photo taken from afar—
a small human form, lonely and out of place,
dangling from below the bridge, high above the river.

Like clockwork, three in the afternoon, we drove
to the Trammels' house on South Sycamore Street—
my dad's dirty laundry from the week before
in a plastic basket, hidden in the trunk.
Mrs. Trammel took in laundry and ironing from people
around town—her back yard sectioned off in a maze
of clotheslines—men's white dress shirts hanging
in rows, drying in the sun, blowing in the breeze
like Mrs. Ruby's dangling father.
Mr. Trammel traveled with the railroad, was rarely home,
and the family didn't have much money, but, always,
Mrs. Trammel greeted us from behind the screen door,
wearing a dress and red lipstick—her blond hair like
Doris Day's—looking, as I heard my father tell her once,

like a million bucks. Secretly, I wished the day was over,
wished I was back home having supper with my mom,
just the two of us. I imagined myself and my mom and
Mrs. Ruby Deschard, riding in the Roadmaster, gliding
across the 2nd Street bridge, smooth as rails as we headed
out of town, sunlight and shadow from the latticework above
dancing on the dashboard like falling silver coins.
My father stood on the front porch, Mrs. Trammel's three
snot-nosed sons scurried like rat terriers from behind her
and out the screen door, and every week my father
gave each of them, and me, a roll of shiny-new
pennies from the glovebox in his car.
The four of us—locked out of the house while
they discussed banking matters inside—stayed
outdoors for the next hour or more, pitching
pennies against the garage door—the shiny
copper coins glinting in the bright sun,
Abe Lincoln bouncing on his head—the Trammel
boys insisting, always, that we play for keeps.

Mark Weiss, photograph

Food Chain

A soft pool of light washed through Colleen McFadden
and me from her father's work lamp, hanging above him from the
raised hood of his rusted Ford pickup as he leaned halfway inside
the truck's open mouth.
Colleen and I sat together on the driveway — a hot
summer night — carefully placing brown June bugs shaped like
Volkswagen Beetles in front of a fat,
gray toad with a face like Nikita Khrushchev.
The toad's sticky tongue lassoed the June bugs in a flash
and they disappeared down his gullet,
one after another, until his stomach was bloated and
undulating — the live bugs clawing randomly about inside him,
blindly searching for escape from the strange darkness.
Six years old — both of us — Colleen McFadden and I were in love.
Her blond ponytail and dark brown eyes
set my heart clawing for escape from deep inside of me.

Except for Mr. Rieder — a man who lived in a small house
on the next block — I was Colleen's only friend.
The other kids in the neighborhood were older, and mean.
They made fun of Colleen because her family was poor, and
they tried to frighten us by talking about
Russian war planes and atomic bombs, about Sputnik
circling endlessly overhead, watching our every move.
They told us there wouldn't be room in the bomb
shelters for young children, and we'd be left outside for sure.
But Mr. Rieder had shown Colleen a room in his basement,
and promised to keep us safe there.

Colleen's dad was a short, leathery man who smelled of
cigarettes and motor oil, who rarely spoke, and stared at me
from a distance as if he knew the secrets in my heart.
He worked hard at odd jobs around town, raised a large
vegetable garden to help feed the family, and raised
chickens in a coop behind their house. He
collected their eggs every day and, on many
afternoons, brought out his hatchet — cut the
head off a chicken or two.

Earlier that same night, for the first time,
Colleen and I had gotten up the courage to sneak inside
Mrs. Swafford's earthen bomb shelter which rose like
a whale's back from the middle of her backyard.
Once inside—my small flashlight casting distorted shadows—
we planned our life together as we surveyed
metal cans of creamed corn and green beans and
corned beef hash, lined and stacked in perfect order on
wooden shelves—a thin layer of rust taking hold on
the tops of the cans—a few dusty can-openers
scattered here and there, boxes of matches,
dried and hardened candles—the smell of damp earth
around us, and the smell from the inside
of Mr. Rieder's house lingering slightly
on Colleen's blue summer dress—her favorite—the plastic
rainbow buttons on the back somehow slightly askew.

Inside the shelter, we had made a lifetime
of promises while Sputnik prowled somewhere above us—
near the top of the food chain.
Colleen, the love of my life, the girl whose laugh
always made me laugh, had begun to cry,
just a little, for one brief moment, for no reason that I
could understand, as I stood behind her, holding the
flashlight in my mouth—the light pointing at her back—
correcting the rainbow buttons and smoothing the placket;
as her father—unknown to us at that moment—was making
his secret plans to move the family far, far away—as he
opened the hood of his truck to begin tuning the engine,
as he hung his work lamp on the lip of the raised hood,
and crawled halfway inside the truck's open mouth.

The Author as Man Who's Eclipsed by the Dark Under the Opposite Side of the Bridge and Sees the Car Plunge into the River in Blow Out

After the film by Brian De Palma

By the time I got there, I knew you'd crossed the state
        into Ohio, & the time you needed would stretch past
a week into a month before a year, before you'd decide
        to have me box everything, leave, give you a time
I wouldn't be there to collect every one, & drive away
        for good. I needed water then, a belief in consistence,
in directions that change with the weather & the clouds
        fading into the black, starless sky. It was above me before
I thought it was teenagers, before I saw the car suddenly skid
        into the water, & froze, then watched the frame of a man
on the other side & another one dive in: the whole time
        thinking I was alone. I wondered—if I'd had the chance
before him—if it could've been me: a headline & photo
        just one state away, all to show you I could begin again.

The Word We're Looking for Is Sorry

It's a child's board game. It's the hardest word. It's apologetics. It's *mea culpa*. It's responsibility. It can be a bullet. Fonzie can't say it. It can leave a mark. Hearts ache for the lack of it. You can't eat it. A man shouldn't say it. It starts with so. It cannot kill but it can bury. Even with vast eyeglasses it cannot see. It dreams. Maybe it rhymes with starry. Brenda Lee's version is a fake. Chicago has trouble with it. So does Elton. It might be buried. It can give. It cannot receive. It cannot patch a pair of jeans. It's embarrassed to be written in a card. If it's withheld it can build a nation. The love of it kills soldiers. There's so much it wants to do. It never gets to do everything it wants. It lives not on the tongue but in desire. It is subject to whim. It lacks vigor. It cannot build consensus. It doesn't know what else to say. Perhaps it has gone missing. Let's give up. Let's do something else. Let's go build a mighty nation.

Wanting to Read Sanskrit

or some other language we might
invent to speak of what we long for,
we'd need a quiet study, facing
south, and time enough to hear
the planet turn away from itself
and grasshoppers bend their legs
to kneel on thin leaves of jasmine.

An ancient Irish alphabet evoked the trees —
each letter named a tree so what was said
was rooted in what mattered.

Sinhalese letters: the tiny bones of the hand.
Alpha, beta — first the ox, then the house,
slaves guiding oxen back and forth in the fields.

What language would grow from the way
you and I bend over the sink, smooth the sheets,
place a marker in the book, keep words
to ourselves? We've always wanted
to pay attention to the curl of an eyelash,
to the trailing wake of a Q. Question.
Quagmire.

But Sanskrit, that perfect language,
eludes us. The language that means "together."
The refined, ideal language, once sacred,
whose syntax is never ambiguous,
whose words hang like flowering vines
from granite ledges, each tendril enclosing
its secret light.

Leaf

I hold
this leaf as if it were now
a stiff brown blanket
wrapped around
a breath of past summer's air

My father
also had dark veins
and mottled skin
as he curled into
his final sleep

his hands
clutched.
The stem of this leaf
ends in a point
of delicate attachment.

I could toss it
I could crush it
it would become
indistinguishable

from dirt but I don't

O how could I make
a proper grave
for this one dead thing
among so many others

I repeat the word
until the sound becomes
as brittle as its body.
Leaf, leaf, leaves, leaving:
what trees and fathers do.

Elegy

—for Sarah H.

On the path to the apple orchard,
We come on a stand of white sweet clover,
Its flowers bloomed and furling,

And behind it, pokeweed in fruit—
The thick scapes and branches arterial red,
Its berries fat and drooping in clusters,

Some green, most turned a purple-black,
Deep bruise set against the leaves.
Intoxicated by their skin's sheen, she warns

They get birds drunk
But for us are poisonous, which
Increases their allure.

Coming to an English stile, she takes off
The top board and leads me through
A brief stand of hardwoods before

We enter the next field. I don't know
The names, but even to an amateur, the air
Is heavy with apple. She tells me

Tremletts Bitter, Winesap, Chisel Jersey—each its own
Whirl of color. Then she quiets and moves
Into the grove. When I begin to follow,

She cuts ahead. At the field's edge I repeat
The names aloud to no one. Mid-afternoon,
Sun angles everything to shadow.

What Remains

The elephants came again last night.
I woke to see them out my window.
In this life, I am going crazy.
I do not mean to be. Last week,
I slept through the week. This week,
I don't know. I used to know.
In the life I lead with them,
I still have a life. They aren't graceful
As I would have imagined.
But they're so quiet. I didn't know
They'd arrived until I awoke.
The five of them gather most nights
Just outside the yard.
I've taken a liking to the youngest calf,
I can't remember what day it is, but I know
His eyes are large and brown.
Yesterday, I ate a little, and a little
Too much. Yesterday, I counted red pills
And I counted blue pills. Sometimes I
Collect them, hoard them. Enough for
Enough. I've had enough. But
I don't think the elephants
Know me yet. They watch
As I sort bills into piles, or
Go through piles to find bills.
They know I've started drawing again,
Watch me as if they know
What I know, as if I've told them.
I haven't. Or, I don't think so.
I want them to know. Too much is built
On what we know. Built and welded
Onto faith, like a country church.
Who goes there anymore? Even my father
Has recanted. His eyes, large and brown,
Were the first to give it up. His smoker's voice,
The last. I know if I approached them
They would attack me. This would be my fault.

My children will not speak to me. When I call
We talk and I try not to talk, try not
To say what they don't want to know.
The man I let in last night, I didn't know
What he wanted. Or, I did. But knew
I shouldn't say. Who's crazy? I'm
Too tired to be crazy. And
Tired of the doctors and their theories.
They'd strap Aunt Hannah down,
Make her shake, and my father and I
Would help her home where she'd
Wander the house. I'd go outside
Away from my father to play, but feel
Guilty for going outside, so would come
Back and listen to Hannah's jokes and her
Stories about how the doctors could not,
When alone with her, stop touching her
Because they loved her and knew
She was not crazy. She'd be telling
A story and start to cry but tell me
It was nothing. The game
Was to pretend she wasn't
Crying. She'd tell me jokes and cry and
Take her pills. They looked so much
Like jewels. Now the elephants
Are wandering the yard.
Nothing changes. I take four pinks,
Seven whites and I am still
Who I am. Last week, I. Last week, I
Did not have a last week, but the week before,
Well, I don't remember. I remember waking
On the floor, on the bed. I remember how
I woke surrounded by charcoal sticks, and bills
I'd used as drawing pads. Everything dusted
In white and charcoal soot. I remember how
The elephants thought nothing of this.
My children would think something of this.
There is nothing to think. So,
I've stopped thinking. This is a lie.
I would stop thinking, if I would stop

Hoarding the purple pills and the yellow pills.
I remember when I was young, and we went
To church in a small barn. How my father
Would take up the aisle to the pulpit. They
Admired that man. They were the crazy ones.
And how, once father stopped preaching,
Our next church did not have grass.
Or a steeple. And no one wore a tie or a dress.
I remember I wanted to wear a dress.
So my mother and I sewed one.
And when I tried it on, I ripped it.
I was too fat. I ate too much.
I eat too much. I order the onion rings
And I order the French fries. I don't eat them.
Well, this is not true. I, sometimes,
When the elephants are not looking,
Eat the fried part and leave the onion.
I, one day, when I am not crazy, will make
Jewelry again. I remember how I made jewelry,
I remember how the youngest calf
Looked at me when he saw me eating.
He did not blame me. He would look
Best in autumnal colors. Die-cast beads.
I've started it many times—it's not right yet.
I'm preparing it, preparing for not being
It. He has lost his tusks, and needs
Ornamentation. I want to say
We understand each other. I just said it.
Funny how, after a while, it is so easy
To say what you don't mean.
Say, I am going crazy. Who knows
Where anyone is going. I remember
Last month. Last month I was happy.
I remember when, as a child, I would
Enter my father's office. He'd look up
As I shut the door, and the games with
The boys at the corner. They could make me.
I slept all last month. I am so tired.
The elephants are coming inside now.
It is time for them. But the house. It is

So unclean. I am unclean. Unkempt. Unkept.
They will think me an awful host.
I need lipstick and to put away
The onion strings, or they
Will think me awful. I must prepare.
Put away my thoughts, or they will
Think me them. Put away what remains,
Or they will think what I am thinking.
They will. I know. They do. I know I do.

Jen Hoppa, photograph

Object Permanence

for my grandmother (1915-2010)

A bracelet of mammoth ivory she left me
makes me wonder if they also filed past
the body, brushing it lightly with their trunks —

and if they went away as their modern relatives do.

And perhaps that was the end of it.
What was no longer seen was no longer
thought about,
           therefore
           no longer there.

Or perhaps, after the crows and foxes had come
and gone, and flies had stumbled out
of the sweetest marrow

             and there was only the wind

the herd returned. As summer turned
to arctic fall, they picked up
these light, porous things and caressed them.

They carried them over the snow plain
and left them somewhere —

white against white, the way the roof
of her house disappeared against the sky.

Lost travelers might stumble upon them
and find their way again.

The femur pointing towards
its vanishing point.

The boundary stone of a skull.

From the collection of the Co-Editor-in-Chief, photograph

The Lovers in Bengal

There was a pond in the village, steps leading to the pond. People would come there to bathe. They would stand in the pond, a *lungi* or a short cloth around them. They would rub soap over their bodies. They would take a mug and dip it into the water. They would lift the mug, pour the water over their heads.

The children would laugh; they would jump up and down at the feel of the water. The grown-up people—the parents, the old people—would make sure that their important parts were covered as they bathed. And when they were finished, they would take a towel, wrap it around themselves—wrap it as they took off the old, wet clothes and put on the new ones.

Yes, as I say, people would come to the pond to bathe. And they would also come there for a social gathering. The pond was, as it were, the meeting place for the village. They would come there to see each other; to see each other and be seen.

Girls would come. Sometimes they would come with their friends, holding hands. Sometimes they would come by themselves. Sometimes they would come accompanied by their mothers, or their fathers, or even their grandfathers.

It was there that they met—my father and mother. My father did not live in the village, but in a small town a few miles away. But someone in the family (or perhaps a friend, I now forget) had told him about my mother's family. "They live in the village," he had said. "They have such and such a daughter. She is the third daughter. The first daughter is married to a Superintendent of Police. The second daughter is married to an engineer (from a good family, Calcutta University). And this third daughter, she is virtuous, fair-complexioned. She has a good voice."

The good voice—that is what captured my father's attention. He did not care about the money. He did not care about the good family. He did not care that he himself was only twenty-five years old—without a college education, with some good experience (perhaps), but not the education, the breeding.

"I am not a nothing, a misbreed," he said. *Misbreed*: this is the very word he used.

He wanted to meet this girl—virtuous, fair-complexioned. The voice—above all else the voice.

And who would stop him?

❖ ❖ ❖

The days passed. My father began coming to the pond. He would go to the office in the morning. He worked for a printing company; he dealt with papers and files, papers and files, all day. But at last the day was over. Twilight came. He would take off his shoes, put on his sandals. He would take off his formal clothes, put on his *lungi*. And he would take the bus to the pond.

The bus would stop about a quarter of a mile away. He would get off the bus and walk the rest of the distance. It was a dirt road, there were often puddles on the ground. But what did it matter? He was going to see the girl—this girl who was fair-complexioned, the girl with the voice.

He would see the girl from a distance. He would stand behind a pillar. He would sit on a bench, drink tea. He would look in her direction and cast furtive glances.

But speak to her—speak to her directly—that was out of the question. How could he do that?

One day a woman was bathing her son at the edge of the pond. The son was six years old, maybe seven. She was lathering him with soap. The boy's arms grew slippery, the woman lost her grip on the boy's hand. The boy fell backwards into the water.

"Help! Help!" the woman screamed.

It was twilight, almost dark. Who was there to hear the cry? Who was there to come and help?

My father was walking by just at that moment. He had gotten off the bus and was walking towards the pond. He was walking there for the same reason that he always walked: in hope of seeing my mother. He would not talk to her (of course not), he would not dare to come close to her. But he would see her from a distance.

He would espy her and he would dream. Dream of the day that they would be together. Dream of the day that they would be married!

My father was walking by, he heard the screams. He threw off his sandals and jumped into the water.

No sign of the boy.

My father swam and swam. He raised his head to get air. He dove down again and again.

At last he found the boy. The boy was splashing around trying to stay afloat. The water at that point was about six feet deep. It was not too difficult to get hold of the boy, to drag him to the pond's edge.

A crowd had gathered on the bank of the pond. They oohed, they aahed. Some of them cheered. The adulation that they poured on my father!

"God will bless you," the mother of the boy said.

"You are a saint," she said.

The others joined in. "A saint," they said. "A saint to surpass other saints."

My father was embarrassed. For all his bluster and confidence he was still, deep inside, a timid man. He blushed. All this attention—for what?

And there, in the distance, he saw her. The girl. She had short black hair. She was dressed in a lime-green outfit: green pajamas, a green skirt. A long white scarf thrown backwards over her shoulders. She was looking at him.

Looking.

There was, he thought, a smile on her face. There was—or did he only imagine it?—a look of adulation as well.

❖ ❖ ❖

This was, then, the beginning. And why drag it out—why make a short story long?

Contact was made. The relatives of the girl approached the relatives of my father. The boy and girl were introduced to each other formally. The relatives, of course, were present in the room. They all drank tea. My father smiled, my mother blushed, lowered her head.

The date of the wedding was set. Four months later they were married.

The priest said to my father, "Who are you?"

My father answered: "I am Hemant Kumar."

The priest said to my mother, "Who are you?"

My mother answered: "I am Usha."

They walked around a fire seven times. When they finished, the people smiled, asked them, "One more time."

"No no," the priest cried out. "There is no need. The deed has been done."

The deed has been done. I paused, I looked at my audience. Were the people still there? Were they still listening?

I saw some smiles. I met, directly, the eyes of a few. I was reassured.

I went on.

My father married, he was a happy man. He went back to work with joy and energy. He worked for a printing company. He worked every day.

Sometimes it would rain. You know how Bengal is, how hard it sometimes rains. My father would take my mother's hand, he would take her out to the veranda. "Usha," he would say. "Look, Usha, look."

Sometimes he would take my mother's hand and go running into the rain itself.

"Stop!" my mother would call out, screaming, laughing, pulling back her hand from his pull. "Stop, crazy man, stop!"

But my father would not stop. He would take her out in the rain. He would hold her by the hand or the wrist. He would hold her and twirl her in a circle.

The rain would fall hard—so hard it would fall. My father's voice would ring out in the air. My mother's laughter—cries, laughter, cries, laughter—would ring out in the air as well.

My father was a timid and reserved man. But he was in love. And love is love. Who knows what love can do?

And my mother, was she not in love as well? Those were the old, the golden, days. What was not possible? What could not come to pass?

❊   ❊   ❊

One day the war came. My father left and joined the army. The Japanese were in Burma, he was there. They were moving closer—to Bengal, even to Bengal. He was there as well.

But the war ended, my father came back.

The days passed peacefully. My sister was born. They called her Savitri, after the virtuous maiden. Two years passed. I was born. They called me Gaya—after the word cow, but also meaning mother, earth: the cow as mother and earth.

They were busy years. When you have children, you are busy, you have to be so. You have to raise the children, take care of them. There was an *ayah*—a governess—who helped out. But there was work, of course there was a lot of work. The children get sick, the children want toys. They want you to read, they want you to play.

Those days, I tell you. They were sweet and innocent days!

God was above us, he was looking after us. And why should we not enjoy them—the sweet and innocent days.

But these days, could they last? Could they really last? God has created a world, He has not created an easy world. Sometimes He wishes things to be otherwise.

The years passed and my father grew sick. At first it was just small things: he could not remember a name. The name of a person, the name of a place. It would be there on the tip of his tongue but somehow, somehow, it would slip away.

Then it would be bigger things. He would be in mid-sentence and he would suddenly stop. He would not remember what he was saying. A person would walk in, even a relative. "Who is that?" he would say.

A few minutes later—even a few seconds—he would remember. But why did he forget in the first place?

"It is normal," they said.

"It is nothing," they said.

"It is what some people do all the time."

But was it as simple as that?

Sometimes my father would go to the window. He would just stand there. He would call out to passersby.

"Hello," he would say.

"Why do you not look at me?"

"Is this any way to treat a man—a *respectable* man? Is this any way to behave?"

The people would just look at him, stare. Some of them had known him, or at least seen him, for years. He *was* a respectable man. And was this any way for such a man to behave?

My mother worried for him, she worried every day. But what could she do?

Sometimes he would lose his temper and he would push my mother. Sometimes he would hit her. Sometimes my mother had to go to the market for a few minutes. She would close the door and lock it from the outside. She did not want him to go wandering off on his own.

He would stand at the window (the one with the grilles), angrily calling out to passersby. "Open the door, you bastards," he would say. "Open the door. Don't you see that she has locked me—locked me inside?"

Sometimes my mother was home and the door was slightly open. She was busy with something in the kitchen. He would put on his robe. He would put on his slippers (or sometimes he would even be barefoot). And he would go out to the street.

He would go looking for *ladoos* (sweet cakes), "the kind that Nanaji would always bring." He would go looking for copybooks. "My teacher told me that I must write neatly. And if I do not have a copybook, how can I write?"

He would go looking for tangerines. He loved to see the tangerines at the stall, piled in a mound, one on top of the other. "Pretty," he would say, "are they not pretty?" "The smell," he would say, "do you not like the smell?"

❊ ❊ ❊

One day my mother gave him his food. She locked the door. And she went to the pond. It had been long—so long—since she had been there. But something forced her, impelled her, and so she went.

It was a cold and cloudy day, not many people were there. She sat on a rock. A bird came and sat in the distance. It was a pretty bird with a long neck.

"What a noble bird," my mother said.

My mother sat there for some time. She was lost in reverie, lost in the past—who could say.

There was a fish there, a tiny fish. "How small, a *baby*," my mother said.

My mother was lost in reverie. Suddenly she was awakened—was it startled?—by a sound. She looked up and it was the bird—the noble bird. It was at the edge of the pond. And it had the fish, the baby, in its mouth.

My mother sat there for some time. It was a big world, a bird—a noble bird—had made the world. And sometimes the bird came. It was proud, it shrieked. Perhaps the sound startled you. And it took the baby away.

＊　＊　＊

My mother rose—she forced herself to rise. And she made her way home.

The days passed, the weeks. The weeks passed, the months. My father was sick, he grew sicker. And what was there to be done?

My mother took him to all the doctors she could find. She took him to the doctors in Dacca, she took him to the doctors in Chittagong. But do you think it helped?

She gave him Teramycin (for the eyes), she gave him Borofax (for the lips). She gave him Silicia, Ferrum Phos, Natrum Mur. She gave him every medicine she had ever used—every medicine anyone had ever used on her.

The people thought she was mad. What was the point of these medicines—these irrelevant medicines? What effect could they have?

But she gave them, she believed in them. They had worked on her—worked on her when she was sick, worked on her when she was a child. Why should they not work now?

It was faith, don't you see? (Or perhaps it was madness.) They were good medicines, they were kind medicines. They had worked on her. And so why should they not work now?

But of course the medicines did not work. The illness was a big illness, the medicines were small medicines. And work—how could they work?

My father grew sicker. One day he wet his bed. My mother had to help him off the bed. (How heavy he was!) She rolled him over and she helped him to sit up. She took her arm and she put it around his shoulders. She lifted him up—he fell back; she lifted him up—he fell back. A third time she tried, a fourth.

At last she managed. She sat him up on the chair. She took off the sheet from the bed, changed it.

He sat on the chair—he was panting now, he was restless. Then his eyes closed, his head drooped. She was afraid that if she left the room, he would fall off the chair.

That night my mother sat in the corner, she turned on the low lamp. She took a pad, she took an old pen (it was the only one she could find), and she wrote a letter. She wrote a letter to God.

It was a simple letter. She wrote it in Hindi and then in Bengali. The script was small, it slanted from left to right.

"Dear God," she began.

※　※　※

The day passed, the weeks (or was it the months?). The weeks passed, the months (or was it the years?). My father went to the window, he stood there. He went to the window, he cursed. One day he said that there was a story—a story he must tell.

"A story?"

A story he must tell.

My mother told him to be quiet, she told him to get his rest.

But he would have none of it. "Rest," he said, "who needs rest? A person can rest all his life."

There was a glitter in his eye, a strange look. He took a deep breath, and then a second. He took another deep breath. His breathing was labored. He went on.

He spoke about life, he spoke about death. They were strange words—the words were jumbled, the meaning not clear. But he needed to speak. He went on.

He spoke about the past: the times in Poona when they owned the factory. He spoke about the past: the times in Delhi when he worked in the sugar mill. But especially he spoke about his childhood: the times in Dacca when his mother's father, his Nanaji, would come to visit. The *ladoos* he would bring.

"He would bring me *ladoos*—they were the best *ladoos* in the world."

"*Ladoos*?"

"I would stand at the door, you see, and wait. I would wait to see his figure, his tall figure, in the distance (the turban, the white turban at the top). At last I would see him and go running. He would be standing there, his face blank, or even stern, his arms behind his back. I would ask him if he had brought me anything.

"'No,' he would say.

"I would ask him again.

"'No,' he would say.

"A third time I would ask him, a fourth. (It was a game, you see, just a game.)

"But he could not keep up the pretense forever. At last his face would break out into a smile. '*Ladoos*,' he would say, 'only *ladoos*. You know, the ones you like so much. The ones they sell in the bazaar.'

"Or else: 'A box,' he would say. 'Just a box.'

"But it was no ordinary box. It was the box with the picture of the goddess Lakshmi on top. There was a string on the top, brown and yellow. And there were *ladoos* inside—the best *ladoos* in the world.

"I would put the box in my left hand (or I would hug it against my chest). I would put my right hand in his left hand. And thus we would walk, my Nanaji and I, swinging hand in hand— thus we would walk towards home.

"Nanaji did not want me to open the box (not yet). 'Oh ho, wait,' he would say, 'can you wait one minute till we get home?'

"And I was a good boy, you see, I was a good boy. I did *not* open it—I did not open it till I got home."

He told the story, his breathing was labored. He would begin to sweat—you thought that he was about to choke.

But then, somehow, he would recover. He would go on. He would take a deep breath, and then a second. He would find the strength. He would go on.

My father told the story with passion. It was a simple story—a story about childhood. But it was important for him to tell it. He must tell it. He must!

❖ ❖ ❖

The story was over. My father lay back on his pillow—his head dropped against the wall behind him, his arms stretched wide on each side.

The days passed, the weeks (or was it the months?). The weeks passed, the months (or was it the years?). My father was sick, he was dying. One day the bird would come, the noble bird. It would take him away.

My father lay straight on his back. His arms were stretched wide on each side. And how tired he was—how infinitely tired!

He would lie there, his eyes open. Sometimes he would speak. But it was not clear to whom he was speaking. Was he speaking to my mother? Was he speaking to the walls? Was he speaking to himself?

My mother came to see him, sometimes he recognized her. Sometimes he did not. "Raj," he said, "are you Raj?" This was his cousin's brother.

"Padma," he said, "are you Padma?" This was his sister. She had died when he was a child.

"Nanaji," he said, "are you Nanaji? Can you bring me *ladoos*? The *ladoos* you used to bring?"

He lay there on his back. And he was lost, you see, he was lost to the world. He would open his eyes, he would close them; he would open his eyes, he would close them. And he was lost, you see—he was lost to the world.

❉ ❉ ❉

My mother took her head and she rested it against his face. Then she was afraid—she feared that she might disturb him. She took her head and she rested it against his chest.

She was afraid of that as well. She took her head, she rested it at his feet.

She liked him. She wanted him to stay. She did not want him to go away.

He lay there, he slept. He lay there, he slept. He opened his eyes. He looked around him. But there was no one he saw—not really—no one he recognized.

"Put me on a pallet," he said. "Take me to the pond (or is it the Jumna River?)."

"The pond? The Jumna River?"

"My mother is waiting for me. My Nanaji. They are waiting—how can I be late?"

"They are waiting—how can I be late?"

On the twenty-fifth of March, at 11:06 in the morning, my father died. He opened his eyes. He looked at the walls. Some thought seemed to cross his mind (what was it?). A smile came to his lips.

He closed his eyes. He did not open them again.

My mother sat there, looked at him. She was his wife—she had lived with him for twenty-one years.

A bird came, a noble bird. People came, what people? They sobbed, they wept. They said that it was God's will.

And was it?

They said that he had suffered so much. They said that it was for the best.

And was it?

A woman came. She went up to my mother and she put her arms around her.

"Usha," she said.

My mother did not answer.

"Usha," she said again.

My mother did not answer.

The woman was not a bad woman, she meant well. But my mother was old, she was tired. She wanted to go to her room, she wanted to sleep. She was tired, you see, she needed rest. She wanted to sleep for a long time.

From the collection of the Co-Editor-in-Chief, photograph

Still Life with Full Moon and Ibis

You know the procedure: you're queuing
in a maze of stanchions and nylon straps, clutching
whatever you have not checked through

to your final destination—all the things you believe
you couldn't live without should your jet go down
on its short belch across the Irish Sea. And this

is evolution's greatest triumph:
this belief each one of us carries
that we'll be a survivor. And there you are

with your belt removed, your boots untied;
with your toothpaste and hair gel clearly
on display inside the lung of a Ziploc bag, funneling

forward, prepared to pass through
the dark gate of the X-ray, distracted
by a photo in your *National Geographic*

of a mummified ibis passed through a scanner
by scientists in Montreal. How relaxed
and almost smug it seems, deep

in its snug wrappings, with its legs
extended and the flex of its long neck folded,
carefully, back on itself; and its body, with every

organ but the heart removed, packed with snails
for the journey into its afterlife. Along the queue's
home stretch on your left is a wall

of mirrored glass which hides, you know,
officials in uniform skilled at spotting,
or so you have read, all manner and variety

of dubious behaviors. And really, it could be any
one of you—sleep-deprived, anxious
and faffing with your carry-ons; in mourning,

in love, overdressed for the weather,
making lists and annotating maps and flinging
little argots in your native language.

Because really, aren't all of us, all our lives,
individuals in places we do not belong. In the stretch
of the mirror's tableau, the world is

what it is. And you think of your mother, dead,
now, too many years—as if fewer years
wouldn't be too many—about how, when you

were a child, she would hide,
between the soil and the lowest shelves
of the rhododendron, every chaffinch and siskin

and sparrow that launched from the feeder
and mistook the reflection of the world
for a continuation of the world while you sat

at the table in the kitchen eating breakfast, or drawing
and coloring your way toward a happiness
of your own making. Even the colors

themselves, their names—Sap Green,
Scarlet Lake, Lamp Black—a world already
half created. *Look*, your mother would say,

whenever you were together out in the garden:
in the window's mirror, a portal
of sky, a fixed portion of lawn and the dark,

green beckonings of the neighbor's leylandii;
across the glass, smudges like watermarks,
and a spoor of feathers: *look*

where the birds pass through
to that blue on the other side, to a sky
undamaged, without flaw. (You can't say why,

when your mother belongs to the past,
all your memories of her are always in front of you.)
There was your first night on earth

without her—full moon, tide on the ebb—
when you walked that widening,
wet cuff of sand as the waves, unzipping

along their length, withdrew and handed over
torn seine nets and plastic and a single
tennis shoe. You remember the empty palms

of clams and Astarte, scattered packets
of devil's purse, slick blades of kelp.
(You can't say why you never asked her

what it was like—her first night on this earth
with you.) Then, a lunge of wind and the high
complaint of a shorebird startled from sleep

and, from the fields, a rumor of coconut
from gorse in full bloom
and the wet sand before you an endless

corridor in which the lamp of the moon
was being carried, always ahead of you, keeping
a constant distance. Where else,

you think now, would she be. She taught you that even
the common birds of the hedgerow and the garden
inherit a life beyond this one; that the things

you want to believe are things
you need to believe. She gave you the world
inside this one. Which makes you smile

until you remember those officials in uniform
trained to decipher, or so you've read, all manner
and variety of emotional leakages—those of you

blinking too fast or scanning the queue or curling
a lip like Elvis. Really, who among us, marooned
in reverie, can't help sneering, or smiling

like that unknown model who became
the Mona Lisa, with just the corners of our mouths
curved like plump commas. But there you are anyway,

smiling, and rocking back and forth in your thick-soled,
unlaced boots, preoccupied, taking notes, building
a shelter for everything you love

ahead of its destruction. And what would you say
if they singled you out; if you were yanked
from the queue and jostled to a table

in some small back room. Because anything you could say
would sound like a threat. *I'm writing a poem,*
you'd say; *I'm thinking about the afterlife.* You'd say:

*did you know the Egyptians packed mummified ibis, bird
sacred to Thoth—moon god, god of divine speech,
keeper and recorder of all knowledge—*

with snails. I know, you'd say, sliding
your notebook toward them, *and I can show you,
where the dead go.*

Cheerful Variations on a Melancholy Theme

1

"Goodbye! Goodbye!" she said,
  as though she would take a turn
  through the unfamiliar streets
  and return in an hour, in a day,
  with news of the fair places,
  with anecdotes of how much better
  it was than one anticipated —
  the wary traveler satisfied, at last,
  with everything.

2

I think I live in a towered city among winged things
  chanting and exultant.
  Above sail the ten stars that whisper their ten-times-tenfold secrets.
  All would be well if you did not call me,
  sometimes, down.
  That crest of moon, that craze of moon
  holds the pictures in her arms.
  You do not need to look, but look you do,
  for sometimes there is such sweetness:
  the bee in her domicile of honey,
  the white bear sleeping in a cave of pearl,
  dancers by a red fire turning but never departing.

Samuel Palmer would paint us, two figures in a field
  silver and shadow, or one figure
  built of what were two an hour before.
  There are thrones
  but we need not sit on them.

There are crowns
but we need not wear them.
But at last we must rise and go.
We must turn to towered city, to haunted stream before morning,
holding some token scented of the other.
No one will know, no one will watch us heading out.
Ahead somewhere lies that still mysterious point,
the axle with its angles and all things
turning slowly around.

3

Here the first snowball peony blooms
      white and sloppy,
      a country girl carelessly brought up
      and yet perfect in beauty—
      here the manifold sweetness of the apple
      bitten the moment after I thought of you,
      as if it sensed remembrance coming
      like darkness through a broken door,
      as if to say, "Oh, so long ago!
      Here, now, the honey and the tart,
      the emerald and the gold,
      rose from the roses and the first sky.
      Here. Now. Walk the broken floor—
      you must—but never look down at it again."

To Aengus the Young, and Certain Others

The glitter in the dust,
        the shards of mirrors scattered
                by the fall of great ones gone,
                        oh, all the heap assembled here

by Cadmus or Maecenas or somebody
        and subsequently blown to smithereens
                by wind that is the respecter of none —
                        this, I suppose, was given me for task:

to gather, piece together, mend —
        razor's edge to razor's edge,
                my blood the mucilage —
                        into something plausibly coherent.

(. . . in the grass, pale ankles moving,
        Choros Nympharum, goat's hoof
                with the pale foot alternate,
                      by the wind the silver shaken and shaken —

. . . crescent of blue-shot waters,
        green-gold in the shallows,
                a black cock crows in the sea-foam,
                      white sheen descending through crystal. . .)

Mad Ezra, you see,
        at my back, sewing and muttering,
                the remnants coming together here,
                      ripped here by fury and delusion apart.

Listen, I have not even failed.
        I turned to other things. Goat hoof and pale foot,
                faun and ingenue found somewhere to dance
                    unhindered by my fecklessness,

I hope. It's not that I haven't seen Him
       on the tilted mountainside with the
             shadow of his swans about him
                    like vague lofty trembling of leaves,

his flame hair lifted and wafted in the wind
       blowing nowhere else; it is not as if
             I have not seen Young Aengus
                    in the oak wood, turning, the instant

before his green-eyed glare would fall upon me,
       emerald shot with fallow gold,
             and in such glancing bringing to an end
                  all divided things.

I have bent down to the ashes,
       plucked up what was beautiful. Escaped
             with the city smoking around.
                  I did not pull together, as the vision was,

the whole and the shattered, the classic and the
       improvisatory — as I must have promised some
             teacher or some interfering spirit that I would.
                  Enough that I have loved enough

to shamble on over the breakage,
       hoof set before hoof, while Walt and Ezra and Bill Blake
             blazed the thoroughfare
                clad in rolling thunders.

Aftershock

*People may be able to go much longer without a pulse than
the 20 minutes previously believed. The capnograph, which
measures carbon dioxide being expelled from the mouth
of the patient, can tell rescuers when further efforts at
cardiopulmonary resuscitation . . . should be continued.*
~Wall Street Journal, May 17, 2011

*I'm a regular guy. I happened to die
at the right place at the right time,*
said Howard Snitzer after he was revived.

Ninety-six minutes he spent without a pulse
lying in front of a grocery store while Mayo medics
worked on him, using a capnograph

to gauge how his lungs clung to longer life.

In that hour and a half, did his soul wander
down to the banks of the Acheron River,
chat with Charon, who refused to ferry him

to the other side, immediately knowing, as he did,
that Howard was neither dead man
nor tragic hero, no Aeneas, for example, bearing

golden branch and the burden of a nation's destiny?

When asked what he was doing there,
did Howard shrug his shoulders
and shove his hands into his disembodied

pockets, then jangle those immaterial
coins the cashier gave him
after purchasing milk, bread, and eggs?

And how impatient did Charon grow

as he counted like strikes of a clock the echoes
of defibrillator shocks — twelve in all —
rocking his usually steady boat?

Is this the story Charon now tells every spirit
he takes for a ride — how the water
throbbed beneath his feet, how in the end,

he rubbed his eyes in disbelief?

From the collection of the Co-Editor-in-Chief, photograph

I was led to believe

you could swallow your tongue
one day waiting for a matinee
with my father, sister, and brother—

the line long, stretching out the door—
as we anticipated the lasers and spaceships
we'd heard about in *Star Wars*—

when another fan ahead of us,
on the other side of the room,
near the heavy, red drapes,

collapsed.
         My dad, a pharmacist,
asked everyone in earnest

for a pencil or popsicle stick,
then incarnated the myth,
sliding wood between the woman's teeth.

I'd already learned by then
how to fool my family,
finding coins I'd stolen in places

where I myself had hid them,
knew, too, how a President's pretense
could turn a nation's mouth sour.

But I didn't yet know you could instill
a lie, believing it sincerely to be true.
And it'd be years before I'd learn

how the tongue of Cicero, cooling
after decapitation, suffered the insult
of a hairpin—Fulvia's persistent stabs.

How later, the Romans,
when they entered the Forum
and saw his head and hands,

red and heavy,
                    nailed to the Rostra,
perceived, as Plutarch tells,

the likeness of Antony's very soul.
How they shuttered their ears,
swallowed their republican tongues.

Loose Stone,

the orange sign reads, as I turn
onto the country road, heading home
    where empty bedrooms will greet me,
left behind as my husband & I are
    since the kids cleared out for college.

This is far from upheaval,
    yet everything feels disturbed,
treacherous as this fresh macadam
    when too much speed meets
the sharp curve ahead.

    Yesterday, our dog stood
at the top of the stairs, whining,
    restoring noise to the floors.
I almost let her go on,
    savoring the company

of her misery, acute & close,
    though her dark pitch
fused with fears loosed
    down the gritty corridors
of our long marriage . . .

Angel in Glasgow

An early lesson: the cold is a friend, stops the mind from reaching forward or back. Everything slows down into *now*. The cold is safe. Minoo lets go into not-feeling, stands outside Tesco's in the late gray afternoon. The air is fragile, comes curling in the mist along the narrow streets of Glasgow.

The Brechin Bar has evening warmth and anonymity, but it isn't open yet. She is trying to get the nerve up to go into Tesco where the automatic doors emit blasts of tepid air each time they roll apart.

There are electric lights everywhere. Wasteful light pouring like gold over the ice and the brown snow, running like jewels down sides of the tiled houses, the buildings, the bus stops.

A man gives her a couple of pound coins. Another man gets out of a car and also hands her a pound coin.

Things to know about men:
Men who give things will take things.
Sometimes men will kill you if they can't think of anything else to do.
Sometimes men will kill you if you say the wrong thing.
Her mother: *Not the children*.

The coins are heavy. They, too, catch the electric light. She can go into Tesco's and buy food. She stands, waiting for the next moment to somehow propel her into buying things, holding things in a plastic bag.

Here is a cold place with ice, many thousands of miles from *here* that used to be home. When she arrived, the church put her with a family: scared-looking old people, who offered her pale biscuits, honey and thick cream. She left after two days. She hid from the church pastor and his wife. She is ungrateful. She imagines them all saying it in their round thick accents. *Ungrateful gurrl.* She keeps to the corners, the edges where the snow melts into melting leaves, and the ice forms over, buries the tracks. She is only one of the many who were brought from Northern Sudan. She sees them, the pastor and his wife, walking with the young girls. Several of the young Sudanese girls are expecting babies and a number have become pregnant since they arrived. The pastor and his wife are always busy. They don't have time to look for the ones who slip away into Glasgow's narrow streets. But she can take care of herself.

New skills:
Scavenging from the bus stop: A padded jacket with a hood under a concrete bench. She picked it up, slipped herself into its arms and walked away.
Stealing from the greengrocer: Two apples and an orange. The smell stayed for three days.
A place to sleep: A shed with a caved-in roof at the back of the parking lot near the train station. Moved rotting coils of rope and a broken swivel chair aside, used a sleeping bag she found thrown over the parking lot fence. It didn't smell and there wasn't anything nasty inside. The joyful surprise of waking warm: *I have been asleep.*

Two girls, baggy jackets, torn leggings, denim skirts, platform shoes, clatter across the road. The girl with a face-chain that runs from nose to ear flicks her cigarette butt into the gutter.
—Well, Tania's not *here,* is she?
The other girl has green-streaked hair and a stomach that sticks out from under her short red shirt,
—We're no doin' it without her.
Face-chain sees Minoo.
—Her. She'll do.
Fat Stomach,
—You speak English?
Face-chain,
—She's one of them Sooda-kneez. I seen 'em at the church. Rescued all these fuckin' Sooda-kneez, didn't they.
Fat Stomach eyes the girl,

—You speak Sooda-kneez, then?

Minoo,

—I speak English.

The girls go *oooohhh* and laugh.

Face-chain,

—I thought yeh wuz all took care of by the church, then.

—I don't believe in their church. I don't believe in their bible.

Fat Stomach,

—Yeh can no say things like that. Yeh'll be struck down. Jesus is watchin'. Me mam says.

Face-chain,

—So what's yer name? I'm Sheila and this is Kenzie.

Kenzie,

—Ah'm frae Glasgow. This old besom's from Liverpool. Loada shite.

—I'm Minoo.

Kenzie squints at her,

—Och, that's a daft name, then. Did yer mam no like yeh?

Sheila,

It's no more stupid than Kenzie.

Turns back to Minoo.

—So you gonna rob the shop with us, then?

Minoo shakes her head.

—I have money to buy—

—Much yeh got?

Minoo opens her hand with the three pounds.

—Give us yeh money. I got an idea.

Minoo wants to close her hand around the coins. The coins mean crackers, maybe cheese. But Sheila takes the money.

—Stick with us, kid. We'll take care of yeh.

Minoo hesitates.

Kenzie,

—Ach, come on, ye daft cow.

Minoo follows Sheila and Kenzie into the narrow shop, because they have her money, because there's nothing else to do, because there's a faint chance that Sheila will drop the coins. Kenzie moves to the back of the store where there are freezers of drinks. Sheila slowly walks between the shelves at the front of the shop. A metallic crash from the back.

Kenzie complaining,
—Whutja put them tins so close together for? I'm not payin' for anythin', mind.
Sheila waves a couple of packets of crisps.
—Can I get ma crisps, then?
The skinny cash register boy rings her up and hands her the change.

Another crash.
Kenzie,
—Clumsy me. Wouldja look at that, then?
The boy runs to the back, red hands knuckling.
—Could you step out of the way, please?
—Step out of the way, is it?
As the boy kneels to pick up the tins, Kenzie straddles his back and rubs herself against him. He falls.
—Gerroff—
—Giddyap li'l pony—
—Kenzie, it's no funny—
—Och, Kenzie is it?
Sheila tenderly folds a bottle of brandy inside her shirt.
They walk to the front, Kenzie strolls up from the back looking like she's ready to smash up the whole shop.

The boy is back at the register, flushed, avoiding eye contact.
—I'll call the manager, Kenzie. Think you can come in here and do what you like? You'll see what happens.
—Oh aye? Wu'll see, wull we?
Kenzie lifts her shirt a little.
—What d'*you* wanna see, Brad Pitt? Ma wee diddies?
Then drags her shirt up to show naked, fat breasts hanging over her stomach. The boy gapes, grabs the counter with both hands.
Minoo's hands are clenched.
Sheila and Kenzie hoot with laughter, swagger out. The boy swivels back to Minoo. She runs. The boy calls,
—Hey—you—the black girl—

Sheila and Kenzie running in their platform shoes. Minoo running in her flip-flops. At the far end of the street, they dodge down the side of a building. *Bank of Scotland*, faded black letters half-scraped off the old brick.

Sheila,
—Who's he callin' black? Fuckin' racist.
Kenzie,
—Well, she *is* black, then.
—She's not black. She's—come under the light, would yeh?
Minoo stands under an orange light hanging over the rubbish tip.
Kenzie,
—She looks fuckin' orange to me.
—Well, she's not *black* black. More like me aunty's new car. Lovely deep brown.
Sheila stares,
—Are them flip-flops? Kenzie, she's wearin' flip-flops.
Kenzie,
—Yeh feet must be freezin'. Yeh can no run in flip-flops.
Minoo,
—But you are running in these platform shoes.
Sheila,
—She's gorra point there, Kenz. Me feet are on fire. C'mon. Let's go round the back-a yours.

Kenzie's block of flats is a dark, fetid building with urine-washed stairs. Outside, someone is dragging an enormous bag of rubbish. It scrapes along the ground.
Minoo,
—It is only rubbish.
Kenzie turns around,
—Hawfwit. Whatdja think it was? Dead body?

You learn that the best way to drag a body is by the heels. You don't look back. You just pull until you reach the dropping place. Then you step aside and they kick the body in. And then you go back for the next one.
You don't look at anything past the ankles. You don't want to recognize the scars on the shins, the shape of the knees. You don't want to look further up and see the lacerated palms or the fingers curled up.
You do this in the morning when the bodies are still covered in dark, when it is cold enough that you don't smell them. Especially when they might be someone you know.

The grass at the back is a dry balding patch but it's clear enough to sit on. A couple of burnt-black bushes provide a little shelter. Minoo shivering. From inside her shirt, Sheila pulls out the brandy.
—Score! This'll warm us up.
They pass the bottle and toast each other.
—Winners, winners, win—ners!

Shouldn't they get inside somewhere? Are the police coming? They don't have guns but they have sticks. It doesn't take much to break bones.

It was a boy, a bored boy. And she made the mistake of smiling because he looked foolish with the gun that was too big for him. He looked like the boys at school in the class below hers. But a boy with a gun is different from a boy with a book. Enraged, he used the butt. She lifted her arm in time to protect her head. That was when she knew they were going to kill her, like they'd killed the other girls when they'd used them up. It had been hard to run with a broken arm. When she reached the Scottish mission she found she was one of hundreds camped around the small, whitewashed building.

But they set her arm and gave her the job of teaching songs to the kids for Sunday school. The pure pleasure, like being shot through with silver: their out-of-tune voices, their habit of examining the ceiling while they were singing, how they tugged at their shorts or forgot the words. How they looked up at her and how she forgot what had been done to her. Until a man, some helper or teacher, came into the room and the kids went silent.

More than the brandy, Minoo wants the crisps. Can she just ask? Will she get her change from the three pounds? Minoo takes a mouthful. The liquid is harsh, but not as harsh as the beer that the soldiers forced them to make in the evenings, before they spread out the women—

Sheila and Kenzie drink quickly and pass her the bottle, but Minoo hands it back. *I drink very slowly.* It is necessary to reduce the heartbeat. It is necessary to breathe the heart back to normal.
Kenzie nods, swallows.

—Yer first time robbin'? I was skerrit ma firs' time.
Then brays.
—I wasnae! No one fucks wi' me.
—Shurrup, Kenzie. She's not used to it.
Kenzie hangs over Minoo. Minoo counts: One-one-hundred, two-one-hundred, three-one-hundred.
—You should do somethin' about yersel'. Hey—
Kenzie turns to Sheila.
—Less cut her hair!
Sheila puts an arm out.
—Yer bevvied.
—Am no.
Kenzie roots in her bag and pulls out a small pair of scissors,
—Come on, Soo-dan. Ah-ll mek yeh look gor-gee-uss.
She snaps the scissors in the air.

Minoo breathes. Fifteen-one-hundred. Sixteen-one-hundred. It's never an attack until—
Sheila tries to wrench the scissors away but Kenzie shoves and Sheila falls backwards. Kenzie with the scissors jawing open and shut. Laughing.
Minoo counts. Twenty-two-one-hundred. Twenty-three-one-hundred.

Sheila tries to grab at Kenzie's legs, but Kenzie swoops forward, the scissors rasping. Kneels in front of Minoo. Snips a chunk of hair. Stares. Laughs, looks over her shoulder.
—She let me do it! Wouldja believe it?

There is no time to decide whether to move or not to move.
Minoo stabs rigid fingers into the solar plexus. Kenzie buckles, gurgling, heaving on the bald earth.
No time to decide.
Minoo snatches the scissors, closes the blades and aims straight for the neck.
Sheila's platform shoe connects with Minoo's hand and the scissors drop, hitting Kenzie on the temple.

Kenzie gasping,
—Bitch! I'll fuckin' kill yeh!

Sheila looks at Minoo.
—*Go.*
Minoo, on her feet, backs away, wants to run but can't. Kenzie
staggers upright. Aims a punch at Sheila and misses.
—Kenzie!

A new voice. Male. The black hooded outline approaches. Hands
stuffed in his hoodie pouch pocket.
There is no decision to move. Instantly, the scissors are in Minoo's
hand, blades forward. He won't be able to get anywhere near. If
she just runs now. If she just runs. The feet don't move. Scissors
pointing out.

Kenzie coughs.
—Fuck're *yü* doin' here?
—Just got off. Y'know.
It is the boy from Tesco's. He stands there, the hands fumbling in
his pockets like they're trying to escape.
—Thought you'd come down here for a quick one, didja?
—Kenzie, it's not like that.
The boy moves closer. Kenzie's face has changed. Softer. She
smiles a little. Looks at the boy from the wild scourings of eyeliner.
—Och, c'mon then.
He helps Kenzie to her feet. Picks up her bag. They walk off to-
gether. She doesn't look around or say goodbye.

Sheila sighs, picks up the half-full bottle of brandy.
Minoo,
—This is her boyfriend?
— She goes with him sometimes.
Beat.
—I want my change.
—Wha'?
—My change. You took my three pounds.
Sheila rummages in her pocket and hands over coins.
—C'mon. Let's go the pub.
I want the crisps.
The alcohol is thrumming in her chest, her stomach. Heart banging
from the attack that wasn't an attack. The rules are different here.

Sheila,
—Look at the state of them feet.
Minoo looks down at the pale green flip-flops against the dark skin, black toenails.
—Yes.
—Yeh gorra get some shoes.

They head back along Govan Road and push into the Brechin Bar. Old men at the bar, pooltable busy, young guys standing in shouldered-off groups, groups of girls sitting around small tables. Bartender swinging glasses down from the rack above, calling an order over his shoulder. *What's yours?* The tall dark beer glasses, short pale glasses of gold gleaming on the dark wood.

Sheila digs in her pockets and pulls out coins.
—Giss the money. C'mon. It's for the drinks.
Minoo hands back her change.
—We got enough for a couple of 'alves. Wait 'ere.

Minoo stands near the door, back against the wall. The police won't come now. But even so, her heart is juddering, beating its own time in a way she remembers. *Out, get out, out, get out.*

Sheila comes back with half-pints of a pale liquid and they head to the small room at the back where the noise falls away.
Back against the wall, facing the doorway, Minoo holds the cold glass in cold hands, stares into the condensation. Trickles clear small, winding paths. That one is hers. The one that stops suddenly is her mother's. Her brothers', her father's, the baby's.

Sheila swallows a mouthful.
— I suppose it's none of me business, but what really happened over there? How come yez all had to leave? They all murderin' yez, like?
Minoo releases the glass.
—I'm from Kosti. It is a big town in North Sudan. It is below Khartoum. Do you know Khartoum?
—I saw that Sudan on the telly. Africa, righ'? I love them beads you lot put in yer hair, yeh?

Minoo was once one of those girls on the telly. She and her mother fetched firewood and balanced 15-gallon jerry-cans of water on their heads. Each night her mother braided her hair. That was before the soldiers came.

—So did them church lot come and save yez?
The glass of beer: pale gold running with tears.
—Those church people tell lies. They tell lies to us in our country and they tell lies to us in this country. And then the girls are pregnant.
—Yeh. It's always the fuckin' men.
Sheila tips the beer back. As she swallows, Minoo sees a thin, pale line across the left side of the throat.
—Someone cut you?
She gestures to Sheila's throat.
—Yeh. Me dad. Got pregnant off his best friend, didn't I?
—But—his friend—
—Don't remember nottin'. Drunk, wasn't I? Me dad went mad. Lucky me mam stopped him.
Minoo is silent. Everything tumbles like a bad movie. Purple-white lights in Tesco's, scissors, brandy, cold blank sky, a man cutting his daughter's throat.

Screech and bellow as something is murdered in the bar. Sheila's eyebrows hitch, one pierced with a silver stud.
—That'll be the karaoke. You ever done the karaoke? C'mon. It'll be a great cultural experience.

She was looking at me, yeh, me, and I could tell it wouldn't be long…
In the bar people shout above the music. Girls draped around each other, *me, yeh, me.* Explosions of laughter. Cheering. The men in the crowd are shouting almost louder than the small, middle-aged man with a microphone right up to his yellow teeth.
Ah love rocknroll put another dam in the jukebox baby

—Let's us have a go, eh? You an' me could sing something, yeh?
Sheila pushes to the front and says something to a bearded man with a clipboard. He nods. Sheila comes back.
—We're on next. You ready?
Minoo looks around for the door.

—I don't know these songs—
—It doesn't matter. Just follow along.
—But I—
—You can sing, righ'? Everyone can sing.
—What?
The music is terrible, painful, blistering. The song ends and cheers overtake any remaining conversation. Laughter.

Her mother and father, her three brothers, sitting on stools, everyone laughing because they have eaten. Her brother has washed the utensils. Mother said, *He will make a fine husband*. And they all laughed. And her stomach was warm.

A girl in a short skirt sings, loud, earnest, flat. And then Sheila is tugging on her arm.
—It's us.
Ooze.
The grinning faces gel, congeal, melt, pull apart. She can't tell if they're friendly or not. Sheila holds on to her sleeve as someone slurs,
—*Whurr dya find thus one?*
Sheila shouts over the music,
—Ignore them. Ignorant load of shite. There's the screen. Just sing along.
The blue screen begins to scroll words. Minoo looks at Sheila who starts to sing over a chirpy steel guitar.
—*Ah trad so hard my dear to show that yer mah every dream, yet yer afraid each thing ah do is just some evil scheme...*
Sheila nods at her. Minoo looks back at the screen. Her tongue is frozen. Someone shouts,
—C'mon, hen. Sing!
Minoo opens her mouth and whispers,
—*keep us so far apart*—
And is saved by the roar of the crowd,
Why can't I free yer doubtful mahnd and melt yer cold cold heart.

She stares hard at the blue screen, mic in a death grip. When will it end? They get to the *cold cold heart* line again and a big man with a thick, red beard, bellows along, a few words behind. This echoing effect makes the song even longer than it is. Minoo watches the man sing, his head up, eyes squeezed shut, and his pint of beer clutched to his belly.

As she finishes the song, she is weeping. The man opens his eyes. His face and neck are running with sweat. Even his pale-gold eyebrows are damp. He stares at her, through the cheering, the clapping, the whistles.

The memory of smell:
Her mother: wood smoke, a sweet smell, body lotion.
Her father: oil, cigarette smoke, the cold of being outdoors.
Her brothers: dirt, trees, small-boy sweat.
Her sister: baby hair.
When the memory of smell goes that's when the person begins to fade.
In the dream, she tells herself to stay awake to remember. As she breathes, their voices come back, their bodies flicker in the fire-light, they move the air around them and she can feel how they *are*. *We are well. You will not leave us. We don't think you can forget us.*

Someone says,
—Even the wee black one's cryin'. God love 'er.
The red-bearded man strides across to the stage and holds out his hand. Minoo takes it, steps down, and he leads her to a corner of the bar.
He orders two whiskeys and places one in front of her.
Nods his head. They clink glasses. He leans forward.
—Yeh sing like 'n angel.
—Thank you. I saw you singing, too.
—Ma wife. She took the young 'uns aff tae Manchester. Might as well be Africa—no offense. Eight years ago. She can rot in hail, the auld besom. It's the kids. I miss ma kids.
He knocks the whiskey back.
—Ye got family?
—Dead.
She surprises herself with the Scots accent: *deid*.
He nods.
—Bastards. In the war were ye? Hurd about tha'.
—Aye.
The Scots word comes suddenly, easily. Her mouth can do new things. She can sing. She can speak the Scottish language.

He nods again.
—Aye. Them as done the war, they got it comin', angel. Don't you worry. They got it comin' bug time.
He tilts his head,
—Angel. Guid name for ye.
Points at her hair.
—Y'even got a wee halo.
She lifts a hand to touch her hair. Halo.
—Ma name's Preston Robert, but everyone calls me Pirate. It's tha beard.
—It's a good name. Pirate.
—Naice the way ye say it. Pi-rate.

Sheila arrives.
—Y'alright, hen?
—This is Pirate.
—A pirate are, yeh? And what're youse sayin' to me mate?
—I was complimentin' yer friend on her sungin'. Ye're nae bad yersel'.
Sheila grins,
—Well, thanks, then.
He raises his glass to Minoo,
—Ah hope ta see ye once again, Miss Minoo.
He shuffles away.
Sheila rolls her eyes at Minoo.
—The state of 'im. C'mon. Less geroff home.

They leave the broken karaoke hearts behind and walk out into Glasgow's narrow streets. Sheila talks about some shoes she can give Minoo. Pink trainers.
—They're not new, but they'll keep yer feet warm.

The mist has come swirling back. Sheila turns off onto another street before Dalreoch Station.
—Well, this is me, then. Yeh gonna be alrigh'? Gorra place to stay, like?
—Yes, thank you. My place is not far.
Minoo hesitates,
—I had a good time. You are a nice gurrl, Sheila.
Sheila laughs,

—I see yer pickin' up the accent. Very nice. Come round the pub t'morrer nigh'. I'll bring them shoes.

Minoo walks through the curling Glasgow mist to Dalreoch Station. Beneath her hiding place, a loose pile of chipped bricks and wooden palings, she finds her sleeping bag and the *Seventeen* magazine she lifted from Tesco's a week ago. She slips between the splintered walls of the broken shed. There's a faint glow from an orange light in the parking lot. She opens her magazine and finds the fashion advice. *It's time to put away those summer shoes. Make sure you store them properly.*
What would it be like to be so rich that you could have shoes for each season of the year?

A scuffling and sliding close by. A tin can goes bouncing across the parking lot. She shoves the magazines and sleeping bag beneath a loose plank. She wedges herself behind a broken piece of hard-board.
It might be the Scavenger Man, the one who collects empty bottles. She has watched him pick patiently through torn pieces of paper, searching for a number, a sequence of letters that make sense. It might be bored boys looking for a distraction. It might be someone with too much time and not enough sleep.

The orange parking lot light is too faint to reflect the sweet-bright shine of the scissors in her hand, blades forward.

*Untitled**

after Doris Salcedo

1. *Atrabiliarios*

It sounds like melancholy
& rage but it is untranslatable.
We will cover the walls
of scholarship with flowers. Mourn the dead.
      (women's shoes sewn into holes in the wall)

The news today: 2,500 have been killed in X
                Over 20,000 casualties broken & returned
                Civilians 10x that

He says we are making progress.
(the shoes are behind windows of stretched animal gut dried & cloudy)
You have to work hard to see what is there.

          ❊   ❊   ❊   ❊   ❊

My sister called me from the psych ward to tell me that the Devil
is not in her left hand. She is not she. The phone line

                  stretches to cracked porcelain, a voice
more of a mewling, a mandolin's tremolo but not

---

*After Doris Salcedo's *Atrabiliarios*, 1992 (wall niches, shoes, animal fibre, surgical thread; dimensions variable) and other installations. Lines in italics were spoken by Doris Salcedo.

my sister. The girl who fed me while the marriage collapsed
around us. That girl is not.

                    I am walking
through a lawn of shoes, commemorating the dead so far in Iraq.
100s of men's army boots & an occasional stuffed animal,
              plastic flowers: a moving cemetery. A side-show.

There is a pile to represent Iraqi civilians—women's shoes
& the shoes of small children.
                    These piles should be bigger, I keep thinking, as I walk
              unsatisfied through the field.

                    What happens when we cannot trust the dead?

The artist fills an armoire
with a woman's cotton nightgown & cement. You can see corners of soft
              cotton emerging from cement, but can do nothing,
cannot brush it aside . . . *knowledge and control are precarious tools
for us to deal with reality*—The cotton coughs *yes she was*

                ❊   ❊   ❊   ❊   ❊

My sister re-tells history—her history & mine—
              until our past is not ours.
I cannot argue.
                    If I interrupt
                    with my version
                              she will turn at me,
              eyes skipping in panic,
her face tense & no
              longer hers. She will become something

I cannot recognize & remember how to love.

Her voice will stretch high & taut
                              (animal gut over a broken window)

& her words will spit out tight & fast,

faster with accusations covering years of my life.

So I say

nothing. Why such allegiance to a past
full of men's hands? Why not give up & give her
my childhood & stop fighting? The radio says we are bombing Faludja.

2. Museum

You must buy a ticket to walk through the Holocaust
Museum. Once you're in, you can't come back
without another ticket & timeslot. *I don't believe*
that space can be neutral. My brother & I take four hours
& skip lunch. The museum is built like a lyric: a corridor
conveys us past the sheer cliffs of another. We move
slowly between a left wall of portrait photographs, a right wall
full of names. Dozens of tourists pass us,
talk of other things past thousands of destroyed Russian villages. Gone.

Words on a wall,   then piles of eyeglasses,

& piles of hair, even higher, mostly brown —

(a haystack, a __, not this —)

It takes all our energy to stay awake & to keep this hair pile hair.

— to resist the clamp of nouns. The fixing of sight lines.

So much depends on where
you stand to look, to lose, we stand back, gazing across

the expanse

of similar versions: the body of history.
By the time we get to the empty boxcar
on the third floor, boxcar is no longer boxcar.

My brother & I walk not speaking to the Mall & devour
our sandwiches. I tell him about the neighbor who touched me
& my sister when we were very young. He looks up,
his face exhausted, rinsed clear from the exhibits: "I am
so sorry it took you this long
to tell me." The space between my sister & me contracts for a moment,

then widens.

❀　　❀　　❀　　❀　　❀

There are so many ways to hide the body count:
contract workers
consultants
embedded journalists
And if we want to see the dead returned under flag-cover?
We must be morbid, insurgents.

& a sister who returns from psychiatry foreign, invaded
by generic drugs, dominated by diagnosis—
& the family—
How to find what the artist seeks (*the splendor of a complete life*)?

❀　　❀　　❀　　❀　　❀

In the gallery she tries to give us nothing
to see—to experience almost, but not—
(a bookshelf full of cement) *These pieces stand as pure absence.*
to leave a trace—

Where do I put the other sister, the one before disease came to stay?
In a photo album, the lines of a poem, a cement-filled bed?
Quantum theory says both exist—
what version of me do I use?

3. Unfinished

She was born premature & pigeon-toed & worse.
Three operations before her first birthday.
"I put her small legs in casts & kept them
separated by a steel bar when she slept.
The doctors said it was a good idea."

Come into this world & —
the body will adjust to another's—

"I raised a girl knowing
there was no where to run.
I believed the diagnosis."

The artist stacks up the boxes in the corner of the gallery. Beautiful
        boxes of dried cow bladder, lacquered & waiting.
                          She stores our escape —
          Look at the family albums.
          See for yourself.

News flash & then gone: we bombed the Kabul Zoo.
The streets are full of wild animals,

                  uncaged & starving, schoolboys
      corner a tiger in an alley,
      taunt her & eat her. Suck the grease off each finger
      one at a time. Polish their shoes with their hands.

4. Not To Relic

    Third World waste is extreme like our reality —
she wanted to make sculpture out of nothing —
             after eight Colombian Justices were torched
inside the court & she smelled their dying.

            She could only make work out of nothing —
so she took objects that had meaning
      to the deads' living & worked the objects until they had no

          meaning, but still this was not nothing,
                    not nothing —

Our ordinary terrorisms:
        to wake in the night to watch your daughter beaten
        & shoved into a car
& then nothing.
      How to build from that?

❈   ❈   ❈   ❈   ❈

If your daughter
disappears, you must go to the mass grave
& look for her shoes. You will not find her
thin ankles, you will not find the small scar
on her left knee. You will only find
her shoe (is it hers? it might not be) —*in one object is*
the dispersion of an epoch & you will
take that shoe home (you will
hide it in your sweater so others do not
know & you can hold the secret & carry doubt's public shield)
  & you will put this shoe in a box in a corner of the attic
  where you do not go
      & not for a minute will you doubt

the shoe is gathering power, getting larger
  & pushing against the walls of the box.
It glows slightly when the village sleeps.
It shudders when you think of it too long, or her name is named
in the café. You have no doubt, & so when the artist
comes from Bogotá you take her to the attic & hand
her the shoe. She tells you her art will take
responsibility for your grief & you surrender —
   In these pieces I see the light of a memorial ethos.
& your daughter is & is & is &.

❈   ❈   ❈   ❈   ❈

I try in vain to recuperate
the irreversible. There is only
history blurred by politics / cataracts of public memory.
    Such pain has no borders & to remember such
pain has no place & time
    so it is all wheres & no wheres & even
the body cannot contain it —even the body—
  & once the body cannot contain
your panic —what then?
     pain leaves & wanders an abandoned house

it is a hopeless act of mourning

what can possibly
ever stop it from expanding
into wind? into a desert of windstorm? & once into landscape
with no language how can it not become world?
           & then, o god, what then?

      ❈   ❈   ❈   ❈   ❈

Because she cannot describe the disease, or the side effects,
it will haunt & conquer.
      I am aware that art has a precarious capacity to denounce.
True: our tanks drove over parts of Babylon.
True: the winds drove over parts of Babylon.
If ever. What happens when we are long gone
dead before the restoration? When will hope be conjured?

5. No End in Sight

Once memory
of the paining is memory itself, the reason
she remembers at all, *I can no longer determine*
where my center actually is — If we are always preparing
for war, for diagnosis, what are we —
to turn this intentional oblivion
                which is no longer present into a still
                        here, into a present

& the artist will create from that nothing,
                 nothing, remember — more nothing —

Wheel of Water, Wheel of Fire

Anasazi petroglyph, Colorado River Narrows

Read the stone, the braille of basalt, the book cliff face
facing this river. Read the years that faced this rock.

Magma molten and swirling like the surface
of stars. The lanterns of storms coming like hands,
molding and mantling a continent, a desert, this shelf.

Writing their letters, leaving their names, making a mark.
Leaning on their elbows, bending to the easel, tracing
the else and still unsayable sound. Hammerstone,

stone chisel, did nothing new. Only saw how the figure
took shape—beginning not with the four, the five
outer directions, not wind fire, earth metal or sea,

but with the invisible, the inner world.
Spirit from which all else is unborn or born.
See how that circle is waiting, needing neither map

nor pack, selling no compass or boots, but like some cat's,
serpent's eye drawing the breath in and not letting go.
A window, door, passageway of unknowing, this

oval round where others have gone, still more are approaching—
north south, east west of a sun that no longer rises or sets
over plateau and plain, valley mountain or basin,

but in waves of water, races of fire pools tunnels and cells
in basalt, these plunges and rims swell with feeling,
shimmers and glints good for the swimming,

where light and dark are *Anasazi*—ancient
and stranger —*familiar*, and one.

Steve Lautermilch, "Wheel of Water, Wheel of Fire," photograph

Cerith Dreams

Say a child picked me up, took / me home, & knew in the bone / I was nothing but ooze, mud. / How these slender spirals glowed / in curls & corridors, ate / sand, & grew mother of pearl. / How, waking or dreaming, my / heart hankered for nails, ten, twelve / pennies, driving, driven deep / into wood, planking, shoring / a deck, dock, pier, shack, boathouse / by the sea. How I came to / love auger & drill, hammer, / sledge, & axe; how the oyster, / scallop, clam became my close / in their solitary ways / mates, buddies, chums. Till I met / mesquite — trunk & wrangly limb / sandpaper bark sensitive / as crepe paper a child cuts / crumples & scraps. Limbs barbed with / tiny tips of thorns to snag, / pillow, & bed the souls of / high plains winds. I came to hate / that tree, seed of an inland / sea burned dry, bred like a cloud / to float on skies a wreath of / kelp, riding froth & snowy / foam, swimming rolling breaking / tides, fighting kite sailing streams / of salt tang air. Jet streams. So / the hermit me emerged — drank / the cup of the unmixed air — / suicide by atmosphere — / & like a snail drowned — & dried. / Only then the dreams began / like hands of bone shaking me / making shapes upon the walls.

Steve Lautermilch, "Cerith Dreams," photograph

Pictographs Somewhere in the Pahrocs

Sam said the archeologist had an old old record
of Piute pictographs in the area miles east
of Ash Springs Rock Art Site and dared Sam
      to find the spot.
We visit, and Sam takes me to the shaded crevice,
a hole beneath a big rock, and I climb in,
and in the blue-purple light I find
bright orange men with long arms,
a sun with rays like aster petals,
and water, the wavy lines, the spirit paths.
Bright as an orange crayon, vivid as if painted
just yesterday, here they are, the marks
a shaman made some thousand years ago, paintings
huddled in the half-dark, or just sleeping, as snakes
do, hidden from the high white Mohave sun,
waiting for someone, like us, to come look.

Personal Ad

It's true, you'll like my aspect. Which is to say
I have great eyes, appendages, and hair, just ask
my many friends. Which is to say I'm friendly,
I bake pies, lend sugar, flour, eggs, supply spark
plugs, the wood glue. Which is to say I'm handy,
I'm prepared. Meaning, I can start fires
with a flint or just two sticks. Like a frog's tongue,
I'm quick. I throw curve-balls, I catch flies,
I cross streets with both eyes wide open
after looking left-right-left. Even in
a one-way zone. Which is to say I'm safe.
I'm ship-shape, sealed, I'm sound, I sound
just like Judy Garland singing in the shower,
or so I'm told. Which is to say I'm old enough
to know yellow brick from mere gold leaf.
Which means I have framed and hanging
on my wall more than one degree in useful fields
like "Bringing Bacon Home." Which is to say
I don't keep kosher or even vegetarian,
I practice non-discrimination and qualify for loans,
which is to say my credit's good and I've got
some to spare, which means I'll give you credit
whether you cook scrambled eggs or quiche
when you want to impress me, as I only briefly
lived in Paris, which means I'm disease-free.
I'm anti-fungal. I'm shampooed. The motor's ticking
under my hood, which is to say time is passing,
which means enough with the passivity, already,
ratchet up the passion. Which is to say don't pass
me up, which is to say you'd best not miss
this train, if you had half a brain you'd call
right now, which is to say you're dialing,
right? Or rather, just open the door.
I'm standing on your front porch now,
waiting for the light.

Before a Storm, Late September

Another wind thick as wool scratch

clouds shadow like grain ripples
like the wheel spoke tatter of a plowed field:

I keep my window hardwood chock-block open:

tarantella wind, shock of panes
crows driven to the ground
broken in half, the sky is stationary turmoil
my head filled with mulch and fresh-turned clay:

I know tonight's later calm
the public house drunk walk
back along the storm-smoothed mile
will bring highwaymen owls
signaling each other
under a gauze moon:

but for now: wind's grit
the dusk sun prehistoric gray
hesitant clouds full drag
like the throatier coos of scattering pigeons

a thud of wind, a shove of wind
an innocent wind, a patient wind

the sky moves coldly
like the rocked vine's drape:

against its low smoke
an ancient airplane's tin wings
the rusty lug of bird calls
the crows choke on vowels:

and somewhere close
notes as plumage rich as fuchsia blossoms,
as orange light on sandstone

I place my cheek against the old glass
smooth and cool as imperfection
delicious as a persistent rain.

From the collection of the Co-Editor-in-Chief, photograph

Briseis

Unwillingly:
    like heliotropic grapevine creep, a tangle of trellis loops
    an olive stone spit, from its nest the sky shell wind kicked
    the mangle of ill-clipped swan's wings:

this is how, the blind man sang, I went:
    hand to other hands, bed to other bed.

My crushed path along the sea:
    a flowered copse that smelled of washing, the cactus flesh carved
    and scarred with the mathematical equations of real lovers' initials:
sun, salt warp bowing, the small of my back: all are war's spoils.

Sing not of sculpted, sulking pride.
Sing not of beard-red fury.

Speak instead of what is lost, what was taken:
the dust of the citrus grove I hid the hottest afternoons in childhood,
shoulders slightly blistered, feet silt shod.

Tell of my hair shorn short when I was ten:
    on a hilltop, I tossed the clumps in the air, strands in swirls scattered
        like silk seeds.

Voice those blue hill trails at dusk, the weakened light that led me home:
the red dragonfly vibrations, pond water gems:
the walnuts and raisins I winter veranda ate, sun slow-moving like a cat.

Remember my climbing the roof pitch, teenage nights, storm rush of birds,
    like the patter of upward rain, like stars that refuse to believe
    their own message: mother unnamed, father dead, husband's neck,
    most delicate skin, now cold as hoarfrost on an iron banister.

Chant no longer of my bondmaid tasks:
    the donned silk slippers, the dropped slick robes:
    night skies prevented from falling,
    the weeping of the morning birds.

Sing instead of how once I watched a bare young man crawl through
       December waves,
his sea creature back and arms, the water shining like scales,
each loose stroke pulling him toward a dawn mist coast I could never reach.

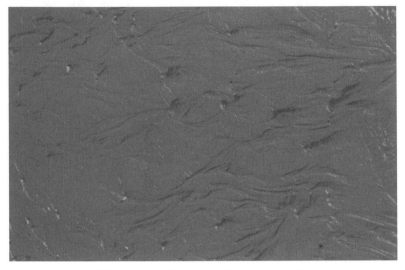

From the collection of the Co-Editor-in-Chief, photograph

The Maenads Go to a Meeting

When we say we tore him limb
from limb, we don't mean it
literally. We just can't resist that
sweet cliché.

Really, it was more
of a dismantling.
He wanted to fall apart.

Then, when it was over, we put our ears
to the wet earth and heard nothing.

[Have you noticed the way the word
hello sounds like *hollow*? If you stretch
and soften the first syllable, we mean.]

And it's not true that we carry him in pieces
like the relics of so-called saints, shards
of bone or cartilage tucked into our purses
or the side pockets of our jeans.
We left him behind.

What you have to understand is that
we're just like you. There are things
we remember and things we don't.
We drink cranberry juice and seltzer
out of our wine glasses, missing the plum-
colored glow of Cabernet.

We could line up here and say
our names, one by one, but it's easier
this way. We find it hard to regret
the things we've done, and the memories
that wash over us are like sugar spun,
purple smoke, like the sheets
of rain that fall gray and glassy
outside every window
in the entire house.

Gretel, After

I think I remember my mother. White hands
on needlepoint, the moon shining
on clean bed sheets. Crushed raspberries
in a bone china cup. I was so young, so
quiet. I didn't know the aviary secrets

of the forest, the way birds will eat
the trails you leave. What I knew of leaves
was only what my father shoveled over the
dirt of a dozen graves, and still I never
wondered what it meant to die. That's why

I wanted to slip my hand into the witch's
hand, let her mother me with caramel.
She smelled of burnt sugar and chocolate cake,
unlike my own mother, who wore the kind of flowers
no one can eat: daffodil, delphinium, the white
hush of oleander.

Sometimes I dream she spoke to me
through her fever, placing damp jasmine
in ropy vines around my neck. *Press the poison
to your lips,* she said, *and the petals will wax. They'll violet
your skin like a bruise.*

The truth is, when she died she said nothing,
just breathed in and out until the metronome
stopped. We turned away, crumbling
bread in our hands, and walked toward the farthest
edge of our yard.

So you could say I wanted this, that hunger
cinched my ribcage until I went to find a new
mother, safe in her house built of sweet violence
and simple syrup. It's true that I'd sacrifice anyone
for the crack of sugar between my teeth.
Whatever happens, I'll pretend
her last word was no.

Hunger & Thirst

JACOB M. APPEL is the author of the novels *The Man Who Wouldn't Stand Up* and *The Biology of Luck*. His short stories have been published in more than two hundred literary journals. He teaches at the Gotham Writers' Workshop and practices medicine in New York City.

BIPIN AURORA has worked as an economist, an energy analyst, and a systems analyst. His fiction has appeared in *Quarterly West, Epiphany, Harpur Palate, Prism Review, Southern Indiana Review, North Atlantic Review, Quiddity International Literary Journal, Puerto del Sol, Southern Humanities Review, Rosebud, The Common,* and *Eclipse, Michigan Quarterly Review,* and *Southwest Review.*

PAULA MARAFINO BERNETT holds an M.F.A. from Sarah Lawrence College. Her work has appeared or is forthcoming in *Rattle, Salamander, Tar River Poetry, The Louisville Review, Margie,* and other journals. Two of her recent poems have been nominated for Pushcart Prizes.

KATHERINE BODE-LANG's chapbook, *Spring Melt* (Seven Kitchens Press), placed second in the 2008 Keystone Chapbook Contest and earned New England Poetry Club's Jean Pedrick Chapbook Award. She has published in *Subtropics, The Cincinnati Review,* and *Beloit Poetry Journal,* among other journals. She holds an M.F.A. from Penn State University, where she is now Assistant Director of The Methodology Center.

ERIK CAMPBELL's poems and essays have appeared or are forthcoming in *The Virginia Quarterly Review, Tin House, The Iowa Review, Rattle,* and other journals. His first collection, *Arguments for Stillness* (Curbstone Press, 2006), was named one of *Book Sense*'s Top Ten Poetry Collection Picks of 2007, and he is a recipient of The Academy of American Poets Helen W. Kenefick Poetry Prize for 2012.

SARAH CROSSLAND likes to write poems about dead people, holiness, lying, and love. The recipient of the 2012 "Discovery"/*Boston Review* Poetry Prize and a 2013 AWP Intro Journals Award, she is currently working on a book about disguises and forgeries called *Impostress*. She lives in Charlottesville, Virginia.

GEFFREY DAVIS hails from the Pacific Northwest. He won the 2013 A. Poulin Poetry Prize for his debut collection, *Revising the Storm*, which will be published by BOA Editions in April 2014. He is also the recipient of *Dogwood: A Journal of Poetry and Prose*'s First Prize in Poetry, *Sycamore Review*'s Wabash Prize for Poetry, and the Leonard Steinberg Memorial/ Academy of American Poets Prize.

MELANIE FIGG has won many awards and fellowships for her poetry, and been published in *The Iowa Review, LIT, Margie, Colorado Review,* and other journals. She lives in Washington, D.C., and curates Literary Art Tours in D.C. galleries (a recent tour was a *Washington Post* Editor's Pick). She teaches creative writing at local writing centers and in private consultation.

JUAN CARLOS GALEANO was born in the Amazon region of Colombia and moved to the United States in 1983. He is the author of *Amazonia, Sobre las cosas, Baraja Inicial,* and *Pollen and Rifles.* He co-directed the documentary film *The Trees Have a Mother.* His work has appeared in *The Atlantic Monthly, Ploughshares, TriQuarterly,* and other publications. He teaches at Florida State University.

KRISTINA GORCHEVA-NEWBERRY was born and raised in Moscow, Russia. Kristina received an M.A. in English from Radford University and an M.F.A. in Creative Writing from Hollins University. Her work has recently appeared in *The Southern Review, The Louisville Review, CALYX, Arts & Letters, Confrontation,* and elsewhere. Her short fiction was a finalist in *Glimmer Train Stories'* writing contests and the 2010 Katherine Anne Porter Prize for Fiction.

CHRIS HAVEN's poetry has appeared or is forthcoming in journals including *Blackbird, Slice, Sycamore Review, Crab Orchard Review,* and *Seneca Review.* He teaches creative writing at Grand Valley State University in Michigan, where he edits *Wake: Great Lakes Thought & Culture.* Currently he is at work on a novel set in Oklahoma in 1955.

DAVID BRENDAN HOPES is a poet and playwright from Asheville, North Carolina, where he directs the Black Swan Theater and teaches Literature and Humanities at the University of North Carolina.

ADAM HOULE is a Ph.D. candidate at Texas Tech University. His work has appeared in *AGNI* online, *Cave Wall, Willow Springs, Best New Poets 2010,* and elsewhere. He is an associate editor for *32 Poems* and serves as outreach coordinator.

SANDRA HUNTER's fiction has appeared in a number of literary magazines and has received 2010 and 2011 Pushcart Prize nominations. Her story "Modern Jazz Parade" won the 2013 *Cobalt Literary Magazine* Fiction Prize. Her novel *Losing Touch* will be published in 2014 (OneWorld Publications, UK).

JAMES KIMBRELL's work has appeared or is forthcoming in *Poetry*, *The Nation*, and *The Kenyon Review*. He is the author of two books, *The Gatehouse of Heaven* and *My Psychic*, and co-translator with Yu Jung-yul of a book of Korean poetry.

BONNIE WAILEE KWONG's work has appeared in a number of journals, including *Califorina Quarterly*, *Contemporary Verse 2*, *Crab Orchard Review*, and *Drunken Boat*.

STEVE LAUTERMILCH, a poet and photographer, has traveled many years in the far West, exploring the landscapes of the ancients. Solo exhibits of his photography have been shown at the University of Nevada, Reno, and the Festival Park Gallery in Manteo, North Carolina. His written work has appeared in *The Antigonish Review, Prairie Schooner*, and *Southern Poetry Review*. His chapbook, *Rim* (2011), won *The Sow's Ear* Poetry Award.

DANIEL LUSK's new work includes *Lake Studies: Meditations on Lake Champlain* and a companion audio book, *The Inland Sea: Reflections*. As well as in *Nimrod*, his poems have appeared in *Poetry, New Letters, North American Review, Prairie Schooner, The Iowa Review, The Southern Review, The Café Review*, and many other journals. A 2006 Pablo Neruda Poetry Award winner, he lives in Vermont with his wife, Irish poet Angela Patten.

KATHARYN HOWD MACHAN is the author of 30 published collections, and her poems have appeared in numerous magazines, anthologies, and textbooks, including *The Bedford Introduction to Literature* and *Sound and Sense*. She is a full professor in the Department of Writing at Ithaca College in central New York State. In 2012 she edited *Adrienne Rich: A Tribute Anthology* (Split Oak Press).

MELANIE MCCABE is a high school English and creative writing teacher in Arlington, Virginia. Her first book, *History of the Body*, was recently published by David Robert Books and her second book, *What The Neighbors Know*, will be published by FutureCycle Press in 2014. Her work has appeared on *Poetry Daily*, as well as in *Best New Poets 2010, The Georgia Review, The Massachusetts Review, The Cincinnati Review*, and other journals.

JANET MCNALLY has writing published or forthcoming in *Best New Poets 2012, The Gettysburg Review, Crazyhorse, Mid-American Review, Ecotone, Hayden's Ferry Review, Alaska Quarterly Review, Crab Orchard Review*, and elsewhere. She is a graduate of the M.F.A. program at the University of Notre Dame, and was awarded a fellowship in fiction by the New York Foundation for the Arts. She teaches creative writing at Canisius College in Buffalo, New York.

RITA MOE earned an M.F.A. from Hamline University. She was chosen to participate in the 2003-2004 Loft Mentor Program and was a featured poet in the Loft Emerging Voices Competition. Her poetry has been published in *North Stone Review*, *DIAGRAM*, and other literary journals. She has two grown sons and lives with her husband in Roseville, Minnesota.

KEITH MONTESANO is the author of the poetry collection *Ghost Lights* (Dream Horse Press, 2010). His poems have appeared or are forthcoming in *Blackbird*, *Mid-American Review*, *Third Coast*, *Hayden's Ferry Review*, *Quarterly West*, *Ninth Letter*, *Verse Daily*, and elsewhere. He currently lives with his wife in New York, where he is a Ph.D. candidate in English and creative writing at Binghamton University.

ALISON MOORE is a graduate of the Warren Wilson M.F.A. Program for Writers and a former assistant professor of English/Creative Writing in the M.F.A. Program at the University of Arizona. She is the author of four books: *Riders on the Orphan Train*, *The Middle of Elsewhere*, *Synonym for Love*, and *Small Spaces between Emergencies*. She is the recipient of two National Endowment for the Arts fellowships in fiction.

JULIE L. MOORE is the author of *Particular Scandals*, published in *The Poiema Poetry Series* by Cascade Books. Her other books include *Slipping Out of Bloom* and *Election Day*. Her poetry has appeared in *Alaska Quarterly Review*, *Cimarron Review*, *The Missouri Review*, *The Southern Review*, *Valparaiso Poetry Review*, and *Verse Daily*.

REBECCA MORGAN's Spanish translations of American writers have appeared in Colombia's *El Tiempo* and Cuba's *Union*. Her translations of Latin American poets have appeared in such American journals as *The Atlanta Review*, *Mississippi Review*, and *Bomb*. She is an assistant professor of Foreign Language Education at Florida State University.

JUDE NUTTER, born in England and raised in Germany, has published three poetry collections: *Pictures of the Afterlife*, *The Curator of Silence* (awarded the Ernest Sandeen Prize and a 2007 Minnesota Book Award), and *I Wish I Had A Heart Like Yours, Walt Whitman* (awarded a 2010 Minnesota Book Award and voted Poetry Book of the Year by ForeWord Review).

ROSALIND PACE enjoyed a long career as a Poet-in-the-Schools and then writer-in-residence for a charter middle school. She continues to teach memoirs at the Truro Council on Aging, poetry at the Wellfleet Library, and image-making (exploring the relationship between verbal and visual images) at the Provincetown Art Association and Museum. Her work has appeared in *The Iowa Review, The American Poetry Review,* and other journals.

JUDITH PACHT's *Summer Hunger* (Tebot Bach) won the 2011 PEN Southwest Book Award for Poetry. Her chapbooks, *User's Guide* and *St. Louis Suite* (Finishing Line Press), were published in 2009 and 2010. She is a three-time Pushcart nominee; her work has appeared in many literary journals and anthologies here and abroad.

EMILY PÉREZ is the author of the chapbook *Backyard Migration Route.* Her poems have appeared in *Nimrod, Crab Orchard Review, New Ohio Review, Borderlands: Texas Poetry Review,* and other journals. She earned an M.F.A. from the University of Houston, where she served as a poetry editor of *Gulf Coast,* and she was a work-study scholar at Bread Loaf Writers' Workshop. She currently teaches English and Gender Studies in Seattle.

CAROL QUINN's poetry has appeared in *Western Humanities Review, The Cincinnati Review, Pleiades, River Styx, Colorado Review,* and elsewhere. *Acetylene,* her first book of poems, was the winner of the 2008 *Cider Press Review* Book Award. She teaches in the English Department at Towson University in Maryland.

KEVIN RABAS co-directs the creative writing program at Emporia State University and edits *Flint Hills Review.* He has written three books, *Bird's Horn, Lisa's Flying Electric Piano,* a Kansas Notable Book and Nelson Poetry Book Award winner, and *Spider Face: stories.*

DOUG RAMSPECK is the author of four poetry collections. His most recent book, *Mechanical Fireflies* (2011), received the *Barrow Street* Press Poetry Prize. His first book, *Black Tupelo Country* (BkMk Press, 2008), received the John Ciardi Prize for Poetry. His poems have appeared in journals that include *Slate, The Kenyon Review, The Southern Review, The Georgia Review,* and *AGNI.*

EARL REINEMAN lives and works in Lawrence, Kansas. His poems have appeared in *Coal City Review and Press* and *Poetry Northwest.* He is a past winner of the William Herbert Carruth Poetry Contest (University of Kansas).

V. L. SCHWAB completed an M.F.A. in Creative Writing from The Ohio State University and is currently teaching at Ashland University in Ashland, Ohio. Her poetry has appeared in *Mid-American Review* and in a University of Akron Press poetry series. She is eternally revising her work and lives in Mansfield, Ohio, with her trusty boxer, Brutus Buckeye.

LYNN SHOEMAKER grew up in South Dakota, traveled east and west to college, and has taught in various universities. He has traveled as a human rights worker and witness to Central America, Cuba, and Iraq. He has published four books and chapbooks, the latest a chapbook from Parallel Press, entitled *A Catch in the Throat of Allah*. He is the father of one daughter, who is the mother of one son, called Gabriel.

CHRIS TANSEER, originally from North Carolina, lives in the desert of Salt Lake City, Utah, where he is a Ph.D. candidate at the University of Utah in Literature and Creative Writing, and a reader for *Sugar House Review*. His work has appeared in journals, his trashcan, and on quite a number of refrigerators.

JULIE TAYLOR spent her youth along the shores of Hungry Lake in northern Minnesota. She studied anthropology and creative writing at Minnesota State University, Moorhead, and received her M.F.A. from the University of Montana, Missoula. She lives in the suburbs of Chicago, Illinois. Her work has appeared in the *Frazee-Vargas Forum, Red Weather,* and a Dakota Territory chapbook, *Trilogy*.

MATTHEW THORBURN is the author of three books of poems, most recently *This Time Tomorrow* (Waywiser, 2013) and *Every Possible Blue* (CW Books, 2012). He lives in the Bronx. "The Light that Lasts All Summer" is the second section of *These Days*, a book-length poem he's currently working on that takes place over the course of a year.

JOHN WALSER, a founding member of the Foot of the Lake Poetry Collective, is working on two manuscripts, *Edgewood Orchard Galleries* and *19 Skies*. An associate professor of English at Marian University, he holds a doctorate from the University of Wisconsin-Milwaukee. His poetry has appeared in a number of journals, including *The Baltimore Review, Barrow Street,* and *The Evansville Review*.

C. WHITE lives in Santa Cruz, California. Her work has appeared in *Match Book Story, Echoes Literary Magazine,* and *Arroyo Literary Review,* and is forthcoming in *The Comstock Review*.

ABOUT THE ARTISTS

ELEANOR LEONNE BENNETT is a sixteen-year-old international award-winning photographer and artist from the United Kingdom. Her photography has been on the covers of books and magazines in the United States and Canada.

KIMBERLY COLANTINO is an artist who lives in Oregon.

GLENN HERBERT DAVIS was the recipient of a Oklahoma Visual Arts Fellowship in 2006. His work has been exhibited and published nationally. His solo work, "image of one," was exhibited at Berry College.

TRACEY HARRIS lives and paints in the Tulsa area. She is represented in Tulsa by M. A. Doran Gallery.

JEN HOPPA graduated from The University of Tulsa. She is a photographer who has taught photography and humanities classes at local colleges.

MANLY JOHNSON was a poet, collagist, and photographer. His poetry appeared in many journals and books, including *All Morning in Her Eyes*, *Present or Accounted For*, and *Every Other One* with Francine Ringold. He served as *Nimrod*'s Poetry Editor for many years.

SHOSHANA KERTESZ is a visual artist and poet from Hungary. She studied fine arts in Budapest. Her paintings and photography have been exhibited throughout the Unites States, Hungary, and Israel. Her website is www. shoshanakertesz.com.

STEVE LAUTERMILCH is a poet and photographer, and his poetry also appears in this issue.

MARY RUSSELL's work has been exhibited across the United States and has been featured in *Southwest Art*, *American Artist*, and *American Art Collector*. She is a member of the Pastel Society of America and Oil Painters of America, and her awards include the Gamblin Excellence Award given by Oil Painters of America, a Salon International 2003 Award, and a Napa Valley Art Award. She is represented in Tulsa by M. A. Doran Gallery.

JAMES ANDREW SMITH attended the Kansas City Art Institute. He worked for ten years as a designer before formally beginning his art career in 2001. His work is exhibited in Tulsa through Joseph Gierek Gallery.

MARK WEISS, an ophthalmologist in Tulsa, Oklahoma, is an award-winning photographer.

CRISTINA GARCÍA was born in Cuba and immigrated to the U.S. with her family in the 1960s. She is the author of five novels for adults, including *King of Cuba*, *The Lady Matador's Hotel*, and National Book Award finalist *Dreaming in Cuban*. She is also the author of three books for younger readers, including *Dreams of Significant Girls*, and one collection of poetry, *The Lesser Tragedy of Death*. She is the recipient of a Guggenheim Fellowship, a Whiting Writers' Award, a Hodder Fellowship at Princeton University, and an NEA grant. She teaches Texas Tech University and is the founder and artistic director of Las Dos Brujas Writers' Workshops in Texas. She was the 2013 judge for The Katherine Anne Porter Prize for Fiction.

AIMEE NEZHUKUMATATHIL is the author of *Lucky Fish*, *At the Drive-In Volcano*, and *Miracle Fruit*. She is the winner of the gold medal in poetry for the Independent Publishers Book Awards, a Balcones Prize, a Pushcart Prize, and *ForeWord Magazine*'s Book of the Year Award. Her poems and essays have been widely anthologized, including in *Poetry 180: A Poem a Day* and *Language for a New Century: Contemporary Asian American Poetry*, and have appeared in *American Poetry Review*, *Slate*, *Prairie Schooner*, *Tin House*, and *Nimrod*. She is an Associate Professor of English at State University of New York-Fredonia. She was the 2013 judge for The Pablo Neruda Prize for Poetry.